GOD:
WHAT THE CRITICS SAY

For Tim Pigrem and
St. Luke's

GOD:
WHAT THE CRITICS SAY

...not forgetting Heaven, Hell, Death, Religion,
Sex, Money, Faith, Hope, Love and quite a bit else.

Edited by Martin Wroe

British Library Cataloguing in Publication Data
A catalogue record for this book is available from the British Library
ISBN 0-340-55687-0

Printed in Great Britain for Hodder and Stoughton Limited, Mill Road, Dunton Green, Sevenoaks, Kent by Butler and Tanner Limited, Frome and London.
Designed by New Era Design Ltd.

Hodder and Stoughton Editorial Office: 47 Bedford Square, London WC1B 3DP.

CONTENTS

Question:
What does an insomniac, dyslexic, agnostic do at night?

Up Front

'I won't be happy until I'm as famous as God.'
(Madonna)

But while Madonna may think people are talking about her more than anyone else, even she recognises that they talk about God more than her. And they've been doing it for quite a while longer. People have always talked about God. God is the biggest of the big things like life, death, the universe, sex, heaven, hell, money, faith, politics. And *God* is the most common answer to the big questions people ask - where did I come from, what am I doing here, and what's on next?

Some people's answers to the question-mark of life have been funny, others have had that ring of truth, others been just memorable - whether or not they include God in their thinking. *God: What The Critics Say* collects together a few of the answers that I've come across.

Although they are roughly broken up into sections, it is only roughly. Within each section, the quotes appear at random, more a scrapbook of wisdom than a dictionary. This anthology is a small cup of water from an ocean of wit and wise words about life, the universe and everything - some of it polluted, some of it drinkable, but most of it worth a paddle in.

It is a collection for flicking, browsing and leaving in the toilet. It is not one to read all through at once. It should appeal to you if you've already got plenty of thick books jammed with words, pasted full of regimental, black sentences. In contrast to those, *God: What The Critics Say* is more like a cartoon book to flick through while the adverts are on, useful for schoolteachers or their students, ministers or their congregations, friends of God or those who doubt that there is a God to be friends with.

Some of the quotes are profound, others are just for the record. Some are straightforward confessions of belief - like Jon Bon Jovi saying, *'Life is a bunch of whores'* - others inarticulate yearning to express something more than trivial about God and the life He breathes into us. Together they point a flashlight on the mysterious path of life, illuminating our direction if we're interested.

I am the Way, the Truth and the Life. (Jesus)

Answer:
**He lies awake in bed at night wondering
if there is a dog.**

1: GOD

"Not only is there no God, but try getting a plumber on weekends."

Woody Allen, actor and film director.

If there were no God there would be no atheists.

G.K. Chesterton, writer.

Gᴏᴅ is like a person who clears his throat while hiding and so gives himself away.

Meister Eckhardt, medieval mystic.

Someone asked (Bertrand) Russell at some meeting: 'Lord Russell, what will you say when you die and are brought face to face with your maker?' He replied without hesitation: 'God,' I shall say, 'God, why did you make the evidence for your existence so insufficient?'

A. J. Ayer, philosopher.

There are 15,747,724,136,275,002,577, 605,653,961,181,555,468,044, 717,914,527,116,709,366,231, 425,076,185,631,031,296 protons in the universe and the same number of electrons.

Sir Arthur Eddington, astronomer.

I think music is spiritual. Singing, playing an instrument is spiritual. It's coming from a spiritual world.

< *Van Morrison, musician.*

on top.
Scientists should be on tap *not*

Winston Churchill, British Prime Minister.

I want to know God's thoughts. The rest are details.

Albert Einstein, scientist.

If people stop believing in God, they don't then believe in nothing, they believe in anything.

G.K. Chesterton

GOD is an elderly or, at any rate, middle-aged male, a stern fellow, patriarchal rather than paternal and a great believer in rules and regulations. He holds men strictly accountable for their actions. He has little apparent concern for the material well-being of the disadvantaged. He is politically connected, socially powerful and holds the mortgage on literally everything in the world. God is difficult. God is unsentimental. It is very hard to get into God's country club.

SANTA CLAUS is another matter. He's cute. He's non-threatening. He's always cheerful. And he loves animals. He may know who's been naughty and who's been nice but he never does anything about it. He gives everyone everything they want without thought of a quid pro quo. He works hard for charities and he's famously generous to the poor. Santa Claus is preferable to God in every way but one: there is no such thing as Santa Claus.

P. J. O'Rourke, writer.

If God hadn't given me a song to sing, I wouldn't have a song to sing.

Bob Marley, singer.

God *weeps* **with us so that we may one day** *laugh* **with Him.**

Jürgen Moltmann, theologian.

Without God... you can't have no music or no soul or no nothin'.

Thomas A. Dorsey, gospel singer.

66 LORD, you have searched me and you know all about me. When I sit down or when I get up, you know about it. You know my thoughts before I have them. You check the road before me, you're acquainted with all my ways. You know my next sentence before it's reached my tongue. You're in front of me, behind me, all around me and you lay your hand on me. It's almost too much to take in, I can barely grasp it. 99

Psalm 139:1-6

God's a funky little dude because everyone's looking for Him and no-one can find Him.

Prince, singer.

God is love, but get it in writing.

Gypsy Rose Lee

God isn't in a pill but LSD explained the mystery of life. It was a religious experience.

Paul McCartney, singer, songwriter.

God is the Celebrity-Author of the World's Best Seller. We have made God into the biggest celebrity of all, to contain our own emptiness.

Daniel J. Boorstin, writer.

Progress is providence without God.

G.K. Chesterton

When God made man she was having one of her off days.

Graffiti

A little girl had just been assured that God could do anything. 'Then if he can do anything, can he make a stone so heavy that he can't lift it?'

A. A. Milne, children's writer.

IN the absence of any other proof, the thumb alone would convince me of God's existence.

Isaac Newton, scientist.

God is subtle but he is not malicious.

Albert Einstein

I believe in God and respect God: before we go on stage we all gather together and pray. We give thanks for our safety, we ask for the blessing of the audience, that everybody is healthy and well and we ask for the strength and energy to go out and do what we do.
< M. C. Hammer, singer.

God is alive - He just doesn't want to get involved.
Graffiti

IS there no God then, but at best an absentee God, sitting idle, ever since the first Sabbath, at the outside of his Universe?

Thomas Carlyle, philosopher.

Once a man is united to God how could he not live for ever? Once a man is separated from God, what can he do but wither and die?

C.S. Lewis, writer.

**Those who deny Thee could not deny,
if Thou didst not exist:
and their denial is never complete,
for if it were so, they would not exist.**

T.S. Eliot, writer.

I won't be happy until I'm as famous as God. I'm tough, ambitious and I know exactly what I want. If that makes me a bitch - okay.

Madonna, singer.

Is man one of God's blunders or Is God one of man's blunders?

Friedrich Wilhelm Nietzsche, philosopher.

I don't go to church but I believe in God. When I was little I had all the usual feelings of guilt. I was very conscious of God watching everything I did. Until I was 12 I believed the devil was in the basement and I would run up the stairs so fast so he wouldn't grab my ankles. I've always carried around a few rosaries. There was a turquoise coloured one my grandmother gave me a long time ago which I wore as a necklace. It isn't sacrilegious to me. I thought the huge crucifixes nuns wore with their habits were beautiful.

Madonna

Let us weigh the gain and the loss, in wagering that God is. Consider these alternatives: if you win, you win all; if you lose, you lose nothing. Do not hesitate then to wager that He is.

Blaise Pascal, scientist and philosopher.

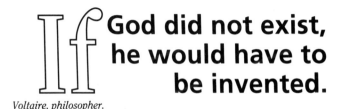

If God did not exist, he would have to be invented.

Voltaire, philosopher.

For God so loved the world, that he gave his only begotten Son that whosoever believeth in him should not perish, but have everlasting life.

Jesus quoted in John's Gospel 3:16 (AV)

God is good, we've just messed up. He's probably biting his nails right now, probably having a smoke thinking, *'What the hell am I gonna do now?'*

Sinead O'Connor, singer.

The language of God seems mostly metaphor. His love is like a red, red rose. His love is like the old waiter with shingles, the guitar-playing Buddhist tramp, the raped child and the one who raped her. There is no image too far-fetched, no combination of sounds too harsh, no spelling too irregular, no allusion too obscure or outrageous. The alphabet of grace is all gutturals.

Frederich Buechner, writer.

THE FOOL SAYS IN HIS ♥

THERE IS NO GOD

PSALM 14 v 1

God is really only another artist. He invented the giraffe, the elephant and the cat. He has no real style. He just goes on trying other things.

Pablo Picasso, painter.

Good God, how much reverence can you have for a Supreme Being who finds it necessary to include such phenomena as phlegm and tooth decay in His divine system of Creation?

Joseph Heller, writer.

O taste and see that the Lord is good.
H appy is the person who takes refuge in him.

Psalm 34:8

By the year 2000 we will, I hope, raise our children to believe in **human potential, not God.**

Gloria Steinem, feminist founder of 'Ms' magazine.

God is not dead. He's just working on a less ambitious project.

Graffiti

An atheist is a man with no *invisible* **means of support.**

Henry Emerson Fosdick, writer.

One who recovers from sickness, forgets about God.

Ethiopian proverb

Between projects I go into the park and bite the grass and wail, "Why do You make me aware of the fact that I have to die one day?"

God says, "Please, I have Chinese people yelling at me, I haven't time for this."

I say all right. God is like a Jewish waiter, he has too many tables.

Mel Brooks, comedian, film director.

The worst moment for the atheist is when he is really thankful and has no-one to thank.

Dante Gabriel Rossetti, writer.

God is a sort of burglar. As a young man you knock him down. As an old man you try to conciliate him for fear he may knock *you* down.

H. Beerbohm Tree, writer.

God knows well how to carve the rotten stick and ride the lame horse.

Martin Luther, Church reformer.

God creates out of nothing. Wonderful, you say. Yes, to be sure, but he does what is still more wonderful: he makes saints out of sinners.

Søren Kierkegaard, philosopher.

God creates and serves, just as I cast the actors, and then have to keep them feeling, happy, confident, dangerous. That Christianity stuff keeps coming back.

Terry Gilliam, film director.

When you see your family talking in tongues and laying on hands, then you think there must be something in it. I was too scared of it. And since I was not willing to deal with that fear, I found the humour in it. I used to joke and laugh at it. But it didn't stop me. I didn't want to get down with all that stuff about hellfire and brimstone. I just thought if that's the kind of God it is, then I guess I don't have much use for Him. And he certainly ain't gonna have much use for me.

Now, none of that took me away from a faith in God that was divine and smart and big, that was a part of that energy that was mine. Because I couldn't stop what I had a desire to do - which was everything. Which was to live. Which was to be.

Dolly Parton, country and western singer.

God is dead.
Nietzsche.
Nietzsche is dead.
God.

God who is eternal, infinite, supremely mighty, does great and unfathomable things in heaven and in earth, and there is no understanding his wonderful works. If the works of God could easily be grasped by human understanding they could not be called wonderful or too great for words.

Thomas à Kempis, spiritual writer.

Is it not a frightening truth that the free will of a bad man can resist the will of God? For He has after a fashion restricted His own Omnipotence by the very fact of creating free creatures; and we read that the Lord was not able to do miracles in some places because people's faith was wanting.

C S. Lewis

I had my own ideas about God and then I had the ideas that I thought were imposed on me. I believe in God. I believe that everything that you do comes back to you. I believe in the innate goodness of people and the importance of that.

Madonna

God's blue period

Not everything has a name. Some things lead us into the realm beyond words.

Art thaws even the frozen, darkened soul, opening it to lofty spiritual experience.

Through Art we are sometimes sent - indistinctly, briefly - revelations not to be achieved by rational thought.

Alexander Solzhenitsyn, writer.

When I perform I always opt for communication with God and in pursuit of communicating with God you can fall into some very dangerous territory. I have also come to realise that total communication with God is physical death.

Patti Smith, American singer.

A man can no more possess a private religion than he can possess a private sun and moon.

G.K. Chesterton

An atheist and a Christian were having an intense public debate. On the blackboard the atheist printed in large capital letters, **'GOD IS NOWHERE'**. When the Christian rose to offer his rebuttal, he rubbed out the *'W'* at the beginning of *'WHERE'* and added that letter to the preceding word *'NO'*. Then the statement read **'GOD IS NOW HERE'**.

Anon.

My concern is to let people know the love of God. The way you do that can differ. It's not just holding up a Bible and preaching. It's by living a life of love and letting people feel love in you and through you.

Little Richard, rock singer.

My experience of God came from acid. It is the most important thing that ever happened to me.

Brian Wilson, The Beach Boys.

God is a living doll.

Jane Russell, Hollywood actress.

When you hold out an empty cup to God and demand that he fill it with wine, he fills it faster than you can ever drink it.

Pete Townshend, rock guitarist. **>**

A God who let us prove his existence would be an idol.

Dietrich Bonhoeffer, minister.

The Supreme Court of Louisiana refused to allow application of the '*Act of God*' defense in a personal injury suit brought by one worshipper against another on allegations that defendant ran into plaintiff while plaintiff was in the aisle of a church praying. Defendant had contended that she was '*trotting under the Spirit of the Lord*' when the accident occurred.

I can tell you that God is alive because I talked to him this morning.

Billy Graham, Christian leader.

Every good and every perfect gift is from above, and cometh down from the Father of lights, with whom is no variableness, neither shadow of turning.

James 1:17 (AV)

2: LIFE, DEATH, THE UNIVERSE AND ALL THAT

The first pair ate the first

Anon.

It is absurd for the Evolutionist to complain that it is unthinkable for an admittedly unthinkable God to make everything out of nothing and then pretend that it is more thinkable that nothing should turn itself into anything.

G.K. Chesterton

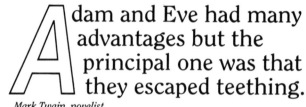

Adam and Eve had many advantages but the principal one was that they escaped teething.

Mark Twain, novelist.

The trouble with facts is that there are so many of them.

Anon.

AND the Lord God formed man of the dust of the ground, and breathed into his nostrils the breath of life; and man became a living soul. And out of the ground made the Lord God to grow every tree that is pleasant to the sight, and good for food; the tree of life also in the midst of the garden, and the tree of knowledge of good and evil.

Genesis 2:7,9 (AV)

There will be no major solution to the suffering of mankind until we reach some understanding of who we are, what the purpose of creation was, what happens after death. Until these questions are resolved we are caught.

Woody Allen

Experience is a name men give to their mïståkE$.

Oscar Wilde, writer.

Once you're dead, you're made for life.

< Jimi Hendrix, rock singer.

Let's face it,
this is an ugly world.
A filthy place to be.
It's a bunch of whores.

Jon Bon Jovi, singer.

Life is either a daring adventure or n thing.

Helen Keller, teacher.

MAN *is not a balloon going up into the sky, nor a mole burrowing merely in the earth; but rather a thing like a tree, whose roots are fed from the earth, while its highest branches seem to rise almost to the stars.*

G.K. Chesterton

If a man hasn't discovered something that he would die for, he isn't fit to live.

Martin Luther King, minister and civil rights leader.

Conversation between Adam and Eve must have been difficult at times because they had nobody to talk about.

Anon.

We should live our lives as though Christ was coming this afternoon.

Jimmy Carter, US President.

I never had the answer to anybody's life. I don't have the answer to my own.

Bruce Springsteen, singer.

The first words of the frog in the Garden of Eden: 'Lord, how you made me JUMP!'

Colin Morris, broadcaster.

Life is something to do when you can't get to sleep.

Anon.

God took seeds from different worlds and sowed them on this earth and His garden grew up and everything came up that could come up. But what grows lives and is alive only through the feelings of its contact with other mysterious worlds. If that feeling grows weak or is destroyed in you, the heavenly growth will die away in you. Then you will be indifferent to life and even grow to hate it. That's what I think.

Feodor Dostoevsky, novelist.

I don't mind dying, I just don't want to be there when it happens.

Woody Allen

Because thy lovingkindness is better than life, my lips shall praise thee.

Psalm 63:3 (AV)

The difference between a flower-girl and a lady is not how she acts but how she is treated.

George Bernard Shaw, writer and playwright.

I think a lot of people are so afraid of making a mistake that they make the biggest mistake of all: they don't live.

T-Bone Burnett, singer.

The trouble with the **rat race** is that even if you win you're still a

Lily Tomlin, actress.

You can't say civilisation don't advance. In every war they kill you a new way.

Will Rogers, writer.

S

elf-decapitation is an extremely difficult, not to say dangerous, thing to attempt.

W. S. Gilbert, writer.

'If I cast my eyes before me, what an infinite space in which I do not exist! And if I look behind me, what a terrible procession of years in which I did not exist and how little space I occupy in this vast abyss of time!'

Bossuet, theologian.

THE DIFFERENCE BETWEEN sex AND death IS THAT WITH death YOU CAN DO IT ALONE AND NO ONE IS GOING TO MAKE FUN OF YOU.

Woody Allen

Everyone wondered how the font was filled during the hosepipe ban of 1977.

When Groucho Marx was asked what it felt like to be ninety years old he replied that it was **better than the alternative.**

✝to die is to leave off dying and to do the thing once and for all.

Samuel Butler, novelist.

When asked how he would like to achieve immortality, Woody Allen replied, *'By not dying'*.

People write to me and say, 'That happened to me'. Then I think, 'You must have a very strange sort of life - because I just made it up.'

Victoria Wood, humorist.

Isn't life a terrible thing, thank God.

Dylan Thomas, poet.

Therefore I say unto you, Take no thought for your life, what ye shall eat, or what ye shall drink; nor yet for your body, what ye shall put on. Is not the life more than meat, and the body than raiment?

Jesus reported in Matthew's Gospel 6:25 (AV)

A Chicago funeral home has set up a drive-through service complete with cameras and sound system which allows visitors to pay their last respects, sign the funeral register and view the remains of a friend or loved one - all without leaving their own car.

A complex system of switches and relays allows as many as a dozen bodies to be viewed. Owner Lafayette Gatling originally came up with the idea because he used to feel uncomfortable coming to a funeral home in soiled clothes. But he says the system has been particularly helpful when the deceased was having an affair and both a wife and a girlfriend wanted to pay respects.

'This way, the girlfriend can go through the drive-through and pay her respects in whatever name she chooses, while the wife is inside with the deceased. It happens all the time.'

Dean Inge once received an anonymous letter from a lady, who wrote: *I am praying for your death. I have been very successful in two other instances.*

Dying is one of the few things that can be done just as easily lying down.
Woody Allen

The man who regards his own life and that of his fellow creatures as meaningless is not merely unfortunate but almost disqualified from life.
Albert Einstein

A fly is a nobler creature than the sun because a fly hath life and the sun hath not.
St Augustine, Church father.

Let us endeavour so to live that when we come to die even the undertaker will be sorry.

Mark Twain

" *Why do we have to die? As a kid you get nice little white shoes, with white laces and a velvet suit with short pants and a nice collar and you go to college, you meet a nice girl and get married, work a few years and then you have to die! What is that stuff? They never wrote that in the contract.* **"**

Mel Brooks

Politics **comes from man.** Mercy, Compassion and Justice **come from God.**

Terry Waite, special envoy of the Archbishop of Canterbury.

I cannot be angry with God in whom I do not believe.

Simone de Beauvoir, writer.

i am dying as I have lived, beyond my means.

Oscar Wilde

Thε late Professor Jacques Monod, the famous French geneticist and Nobel prize winner, in the course of a television session in Toronto with Mother Teresa of Calcutta, spoke of how in his opinion, all our destiny was locked up in our genes, which shape and direct our character and outlook, thus destroying the individual. As he held forth on this theme, Mother Teresa sat with her eyes closed and her hands folded, deep in prayer. On being asked by the programme's compère whether she had anything to say, she replied: *'I believe in love and compassion,'* and resumed her devotions.

As the Professor was leaving the studio he was heard to mutter: *'If I saw much more of that woman I should be in bad trouble!'*

Kitty Muggeridge, writer.

Life is rather like a tin of sardines - we're all of us looking for the key.

Alan Bennett, playwright.

God not only plays dice. He also sometimes throws them where they cannot be seen.

Stephen Hawking, scientist and writer.

Dying can damage your health. Every coffin contains a Government Health Warning.

Spike Milligan, humorist.

Everybody's got a hungry heart.

< *Bruce Springsteen*

What is the thing you respect above all else? That's easy. Death. It's the only thing left to respect. It's the one inevitable undeniable truth. Everything else can be questioned. But death is truth. In it lies the only nobility for man, and beyond it the only hope.

James Dean, actor.

Life is like a sewer. What you get out of it depends on what you put into it.

Tom Lehrer, songwriter.

Death is psychosomatic.

Charles Manson, murderer.

The idea of a good society is something you do not need a religion and eternal punishment to buttress; you need a religion if you are terrified of death.

Gore Vidal, writer.

Death does not take the old but the ripe.

Russian proverb

We discovered early on in life that to go on living was the only way to survive.

Groucho Marx, comedian.

Father Andrew was the BBC's adviser on Roman Catholic affairs. A producer who was planning programmes on the subject wrote asking how he could ascertain the official Roman Catholic view of heaven and hell. The answering memorandum contained just one word, 'Die'.

Paul Bussard, writer.

All criminals turn preachers when they are under the gallows.

Italian proverb

People expect you as a believer to have all the answers when really all you get is another set of questions.

Bono, rock singer.

Life is a *tragedy* when seen in close-up but a *comedy* in l o n g - s h o t .

Charlie Chaplin, actor.

Someone said that the mind is a marvellous instrument. Unfortunately it did not come with instructions. We could say the same for life. All of life. And the more we miss the key to living a full life, the more people invent guide books to tell us how to 'find life'.

Kurt Vonnegut, novelist.

Christ himself was obviously not at peace with nature, any more than he was at peace with human nature. He often acted in open defiance of the 'majesty' of creation. When the storm arose on Gennesaret he did not bid the disciple to humble themselves devoutly before the 'great Being' who was trying to drown them. He lashed back at the elements from his bridgehead in the divine kingdom: 'Be still...' All natural catastrophes are symptoms of nature's sickness - fevers, vomits, shiverings: they are not growing pains through which God is slowly evolving a perfect world, but mere reminders that we live in an enemy-occupied zone and that in so far as we are subject to its laws we share its tragedy.

Jack Clemo, poet and writer.

There's no bad publicity except an obituary.

Brendan Behan, writer.

He had decided to live for ever or die in the attempt.

Joseph Heller

Some luck lies in not getting what you thought you wanted but getting what you have, which once you have it you may be smart enough to see is what you would have wanted had you known.

Garrison Keillor, novelist.

Live fast, die young and leave a good-looking corpse.

James Dean

Owing to lack of interest, tomorrow has been cancelled.

Graffiti

Parishioners are requested to cut the grass around their own graves.

Parish magazine

A single death is a tragedy, a million deaths is a statistic.

Joseph Stalin, Soviet leader.

I would enjoy the day more
if it started later.

Graffiti

I am the Way, the Truth and the Life.

Jesus

Life is a ➡ maze in which we take the ➡ wrong ✦ turning before we have learnt to ✦ walk.

Cyril Connolly, journalist.

Here lie I, Martin Elginbrodde;
Hae mercy o' my soul, Lord God,
As I would do, were I Lord God
And Ye were Martin Elginbrodde.

Epitaph in Elgin Cathedral

3: FOLKS

There are only three kinds of persons; those who serve God, having found Him; others who are occupied in seeking Him, not having found Him; while the remainder live without seeking Him and without having found Him. *The first* are reasonable and happy, *the last* are foolish and unhappy; *those between* are unhappy and reasonable.

Blaise Pascal

What a piece of work is a man! how noble in reason! how infinite in faculties! in form and moving how express and admirable! in action how like an angel, in apprehension how like a god!

William Shakespeare, playwright and poet.

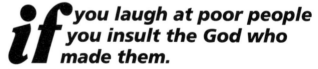 **you laugh at poor people you insult the God who made them.**

Proverbs 17:5

Giving money and power to government is like giving whiskey and car keys to teenage boys.

P. J. O'Rourke

There is only one thing in the world worse than being talked about, and that is not being talked about.

Oscar Wilde

Everyone's got a hunger, a hunger they can't resist. There's so much that you want, you deserve much more than this.

Bruce Springsteen

A man was beaten up by gangsters on the road to Jericho. He lay there, half dead, robbed of all his money, groaning in agony. A priest came along and passed by on the other side. A Levite came along and passed by on the other side. Finally, a social worker came along, looked at the man and said: "Whoever did this needs help."

Murray Watts, writer.

According to a recent study, when Elvis Presley was alive there were 34 Elvis impersonators. Now there are 8,029. The report calculated that at the current rate, one out of every five people on earth will be an Elvis impersonator by the year 2037.

an empty Belly has no ears
— AFRICAN PROVERB

Every ⑤ seconds a person dies of hunger.

We make our friends, make our enemies but God makes our next-door neighbours.
G.K. Chesterton

If a man is centred upon himself the smallest risk is too great for him, because both success and failure can destroy him. If he is centred upon God, then no risk is too great, because success is already guaranteed - the successful union of creator and creature, beside which everything else is meaningless.
Morris West, novelist.

And God spoke all these words:

"I am the Lord your God who brought you out of Egypt, out of the land of slavery.

"You shall have no other gods before me.

"You shall not make for yourself an idol in the form of anything in heaven above or on the earth below.

"You shall not bow down to them or worship them; for I am a jealous God, punishing the children for the sin of the fathers to the third and fourth generation of those who hate me but showing love to a thousand generations of those who keep my commandments.

"You shall not misuse the name of the Lord your God, for the Lord will not hold anyone guiltless who misuses his name.

"Remember the Sabbath day by keeping it holy.

"Honour your father and mother so that you may live long in the land the Lord your God is giving you.

"You shall not murder.

"You shall not commit adultery.

"You shall not steal.

"You shall not give false testimony against your neighbour.

"You shall not covet your neighbour's house or anything that belongs to your neighbour."

The Ten Commandments, Exodus 20:1ff

You cannot develop people - you must allow people to develop themselves.

President Nyerere of Tanzania.

Government is so tedious that sometimes you wonder if the government isn't being boring on purpose.

P. J. O'Rourke

There is no such thing as society.

Margaret Thatcher, British Prime Minister.

No man's really any good till he knows how bad he is, or might be; till he's realised how much right he has to all the snobbery, and sneering and talking about 'criminals' as if they were apes in a forest ten thousand miles away; till he's got rid of all the dirty self-deception of talking about low types and deficient skulls; till he's squeezed out of his soul the last drop of the oil of the Pharisees; till his only hope is somehow or other to have captured one criminal and kept him safe and sane under his own hat.

G.K. Chesterton

If God created all men equal, who do you trust?

Joan Collins, actress.

YOU cannot bring about prosperity by discouraging thrift. You cannot help the wage-earner by pulling down the wage-payer. You cannot further the Brotherhood of Man by encouraging class-hatred. You cannot help the poor by destroying the rich. You cannot keep out of trouble by spending more than you earn. You cannot build character and courage by taking away a man's initiative. You cannot help men permanently by doing for them what they could and should do for themselves.

Abraham Lincoln, US President.

The optimist believes we live in the best of all possible worlds. The pessimist fears this is true.

Anon.

Life is long when you're lonely.

Morrissey, pop singer.

Man is God's image; but a poor man is Christ's stamp to boot.

George Herbert, poet and writer.

To be held in the heart of a friend is to be a King.

Bruce Cockburn, singer.

Renew your hope; love your family. Raise your children, don't abandon them. Cats raise kittens. Dogs raise puppies. Eagles raise their eaglets. Surely man can raise his babies. You have not earned the right not to raise your children. You have not earned the right to do less than your best. Though your knees may buckle sometimes, you never earn the right to surrender.

Jesse Jackson, US politician.

The primary form of love in social organisations is justice.

William Temple, Archbishop of Canterbury.

No one can celebrate a genuine
Christmas without being truly poor.
The self-sufficient,
the proud,
those who, because they have everything,
look down on others,
those who have no need even of God -
for them there will be no Christmas
Only the poor,
the hungry
those who need someone to come on their
behalf
will have that someone
That someone is God.
Emmanuel.
God-with-us.
Without poverty of spirit
there can be no abundance of God.
Oscar Romero, Archbishop of San Salvador.

We must recognise that the motives
and forces behind racism are the
anti-Christ, denying that man is made in
the divine image.
Bishop Trevor Huddleston

There is sufficient for the
world's need, but not for
the world's greed.
Mahatma Gandhi, philosopher and politician.

The world rebelled against the
Golden Rule of Christianity; and
found itself helpless under the
Brazen Rule of commerce and
the Iron Rule of war.
G.K. Chesterton

Headless Body Found in Topless Bar

American newspaper headline

We speak the language of Nothing to Lose.

Graffiti

I hear and I forget,
see and I remember,
do and I understand.

Chinese proverb

Imagination is more important than **knowledge.**

Albert Einstein

'Truth about society is best known at the bottom.'

Jim Wallis

*Must the hunger become **anger** and the **anger** become **fury** before anything will be done?*

John Steinbeck, novelist.

Freddie Starr Ate My Hamster

Headline in British newspaper

Man finds it hard to get what he wants because he does not want the best; God finds it hard to give, because He would give the best and man will not take it.

George MacDonald, minister and novelist.

The question to be asked is not what we should give to the poor but when we will stop taking from the poor.

Jim Wallis

I couldn't live without work. That's what makes me so sympathetic to those people who are unemployed. I don't know how they live without working.

Margaret Thatcher

I think society has suffered considerably through ignoring God. It's plain for everyone to see if they open their eyes and look around. God stands against pornography, illegal drug-taking, lack of decency etcetera and because large chunks of society ignore God, they condone these things. I'm not a prude but if we read the Bible and find out God's plan for us as his children, we can see that society as a whole is falling short. You see, two of the most important commandments are to love God with all our heart and to love our neighbour as ourselves.

Bobby Ball, comedian.

There are great men who make everyone feel small. But the real great man is the man who makes every man feel great.

G.K. Chesterton

God is on the side of the poor just because He is not biased, for he is the God of impartial justice.

Ron Sider, writer.

Revolutions have never lightened the burden of tyranny, they have only shifted it to another shoulder.

George Bernard Shaw

When I give food to the poor they call me a saint. When I ask why the poor have no food they call me a communist.

Dom Helder Camara, Brazilian archbishop.

Some people think it is difficult to be a Christian and to laugh, but I think it's the other way around. God writes a lot of comedy, it's just that he has so many bad actors.

Garrison Keillor

True peace is not merely the absence of tension; it is the presence of justice.

Martin Luther King

People don't care how much you know, until they know how much you care.

John Powell, spiritual writer.

When asked what he thought of Western civilisation, Mahatma Gandhi replied that he thought it would be a good idea.

A **good deed never goes unpunished.**

Oscar Wilde

Fame, Fame, fatal fame. It can play hideous tricks on the brain but I'd still rather be famous than righteous or holy any day.

< Morrissey

mother Teresa never reads a newspaper, never listens to a radio and never watches television...so she has a pretty good idea of what is going on in the world.

Malcolm Muggeridge, writer and broadcaster.

Those who are comfortable, those who have possessions and position cry 'Peace'. Those who are uncomfortable, those who have not, cry 'Justice'.

Andrew Kirk, writer.

If you put an end to oppression, to every gesture of contempt, and to every evil word; if you give food to the hungry and satisfy those who are in need, then the darkness around you will turn to the brightness of noon.

Isaiah 58:9ff

If you are not part of the **solution**, then you are part of the **problem.**

Eldridge Cleaver, US political activist.

In God's eyes there are no redundant people.

Jim Wallis

Authority has always attracted the lowest elements in the human race. All through history mankind has been bullied by scum... Each government is a parliament of whores. The trouble is, in a democracy the whores are us.

P. J. O'Rourke

My own commitment is neither to liberalism nor to Marxism, but to a curious idea put about by a carpenter turned dissident in Palestine that the test of our humanity is to be found in how we treat our enemies.

Paul Oestreicher, priest.

Economics are the method. The object is to change the heart and soul.

Margaret Thatcher

You say grace before meals. Alright but I say grace before the concert and the opera, and grace before the play and pantomine and grace before I open a book and grace before sketching, painting, swimming, fencing, boxing, walking, playing, dancing, and grace before I dip the pen in ink.

G.K. Chesterton

Everything in me wants to move upward. Downward mobility with Jesus goes radically against my inclinations, against the advice of the world surrounding me and against the culture of which I am a part.

Henri Nouwen, spiritual writer.

A Napoleon, a Churchill, a Roosevelt can feel themselves to be successful, but never a Socrates, a Pascal, a Blake.

Malcolm Muggeridge

By blood and origin I am all Albanian.
My citizenship is Indian. I am a Catholic nun.
As to my calling I belong to the whole world.
As to my heart, I belong entirely to Jesus.

Mother Teresa of Calcutta

Strange religious practices
No 143

4: MARRIAGE AND, ER, SEX

The Lord God said, "It is not good for the man to be alone. I will make a helper suitable for him."

Genesis 2:18

It is now quite lawful for a Catholic woman to avoid pregnancy by a resort to mathematics, though she is still forbidden to resort to physics and chemistry.

H.L. Mencken, US journalist.

When I was tiny my grandmother used to beg me not to go with boys, to love Jesus and be a good girl. I grew up with two images of women: the Virgin and the whore.

Madonna

Contraceptives should be used on every conceivable occasion.

Spike Milligan

Sex is the mysticism of materialism and the only possible religion in a materialistic society.
Malcolm Muggeridge

We have a sexy God and a sexy religion and a very sexy leader. If you don't like sex, you better get out while you can.
Moses David (Berg), leader of Children of God.

I'm a wonderful housekeeper.
Every time I'm divorced
I keep the house.
Zsa Zsa Gabor, Hollywood actress.

It's just as Christian to get down on your knees for sex as it is for religion.
Larry Flynt, publisher.

Some people need cheap sex, instant selfish gratification. Fine. But it makes me more miserable than ever.
John Lydon (formerly Rotten) of The Sex Pistols.

The husband should fulfil his marital duty to his wife and likewise the wife to her husband. The wife's body does not belong to her alone but also to her husband. In the same way, the husband's body does not belong to him alone but also to his wife. Do not deprive each other except by mutual consent and for a time, so that you may devote yourselves to prayer. Then come together again so that Satan will not tempt you because of your lack of self-control.
Paul the Apostle in his first letter to the Church at Corinth, 7:3ff (NIV)

I don't want to buy pornographic pictures. I don't even own a pornograph.

Graffiti

It has been said that a bride's attitude towards her betrothed can be summed up in three words: Aisle. Altar. Hymn.

Frank Muir, broadcaster.

A kiss that speaks volumes is seldom a first edition.

Anon.

My brain: it's my second favourite organ.

Woody Allen

THE ONLY GROUNDS 4 DIVORCE IN CALIFORNIA ARE MARRIAGE

CHER.

I used to be Snow White...but I drifted.
Mae West, actress.

Let him kiss me with the kisses of his mouth —
*   for your love is more delightful than wine.*
Pleasing is the fragrance of your perfumes
*   your name is like perfume poured out.*
*   No wonder the maidens love you!*
Take me away with you — let us hurry!
*   Let the king bring me into his chambers.*
The Song of Songs, 1:1ff(NIV)

Sexual harassment at work, is it a problem for the self-employed?
Victoria Wood

Human beings are the only creatures who can talk while making love and they are the only ones who can talk about it afterwards.
Lewis Smedes, writer.

Marriage should be honoured by all, and the marriage bed kept pure, for God will judge the adulterer and all the sexually immoral.
Hebrews 13:4 (NIV)

I definitely have the utmost respect for women, because my mother's a woman.

L.L. Cool J., rap singer.

One sentence will suffice for modern man: he fornicated and read the newspapers. After that, the subject, is, in my opinion, exhausted.

Albert Camus, writer.

*I say I don't sleep with **married men**. But what I mean is that I don't sleep with **happily married men.***

Britt Ekland, actress.

Love starts when you sink into his arms and ends with your arms in his sink.

Graffiti

I want to tell you a terrific story about oral contraception. I asked this girl to sleep with me and she said, 'No'.

Woody Allen

Sex Appeal. Please give generously.

Graffiti

I am a more virtuous man than President Kennedy or President Bush, two notorious philanderers.
Saddam Hussein, Iraqi leader.

Lust is the craving for salt of a man who is dying of thirst.
Frederich Buechner

One doesn't have to get anywhere in marriage. It's not a public conveyance.
Iris Murdoch, novelist.

I have this overwhelming desire to return to the womb - *any womb.*
Woody Allen

5: RELIGION AND THE RELIGIOUS

No-one can understand mankind without understanding the faiths of humanity. Sometimes naive, sometimes penetratingly noble, sometimes crude, sometimes subtle, sometimes cruel, sometimes suffused by an overpowering gentleness and love, sometimes world-affirming, sometimes negating the world, sometimes inward-looking, sometimes universalistic and missionary minded, sometimes shallow and often profound - religion has permeated human life since early and obscure times.

Ninian Smart, anthropologist.

Religion that God our father accepts as pure and faultless is this: to look after orphans and widows in their distress and to keep oneself from being polluted by the world.

James, 1:27 (NIV)

Religions die when they are proved to be true. Science is the record of dead religions.

Oscar Wilde

I am a seriously lapsed Catholic. It was at the usual time, 10, 11, 12, after being forced to go to church and never understanding why and never enjoying it, seeing so many negative things and realising somehow that it wasn't for me. I can only have faith in things I see.
Morrissey

The first requisite for the happiness of the people is the abolition of religion.

Karl Marx

You know what a lot of religious people are like? They are like a lot of people sitting around a railroad station thinking they are on a train. Everybody is talking about travel, and you hear the names of stations and you have got tickets and there is the smell of baggage around you and a great deal of stir and if you sit there long enough you almost think you are on a train. But you are not. You only start to get converted at that point where you get on the train and get pulled out of the station. And you do get pulled out; you do not walk out.
Sam Shoemaker, minister.

Faith is such a personal thing... whatever brings you that particular faith in yourself I think is important, but I'm really pretty outside the whole thing myself. That just didn't seem to be it for me.

Once I pulled myself out from the Catholic school in the fifties, finding that place in some orthodox religious situation is just not something that came to me or even an approach I would take toward solving my own particular problems or questions about what life is all about. I guess for me it's all the unanswered things that are important. It's the holes, the mysteries, that seem to be where it is. People use the cloak of spirituality as a controlling device. That just strikes me as false. Basically that's how it was with me as a child. There was not an interest in bringing me closer to what God really is. It was really used purely as a controlling device by people who had it used on them in that fashion. By the time I got to be thirteen I had had enough. I just told my parents, "No More".

And I always felt like that spiritual thing has run through all my music. Certainly 'Born to Run' is, 'Nebraska' is. It's the perversion of religion and spirituality into superstitions. That's what it was for me.

Bruce Springsteen

'EVERY DAY PEOPLE ARE STRAYING AWAY FROM CHURCH AND GOING BACK TO GOD'

LENNY BRUCE

For Religion all men are equal as all pennies are equal, because the only value in any of them is that they bear the image of the king.

G.K. Chesterton

Science *without* **religion** is lame, **religion** *without* science is blind.

Albert Einstein

Rock 'n' roll was my religion for a long time.

Pete Townshend

I believe that the Jews have made a contribution to the human condition out of all proportion to their numbers: I believe them to be an immense people. Not only have they supplied the world with two leaders of the stature of Jesus Christ and Karl Marx, but they have even indulged in the luxury of following neither one nor the other.

Peter Ustinov, actor.

We do not want a religion that is right where we are right. What we want is a religion that is right where we are wrong.

G.K. Chesterton

Graffiti

The Jews and Arabs should sit down and settle their differences like good Christians.

Warren Austin, US diplomat.

Religion is the fashionable substitute for belief.
Oscar Wilde

I loved nuns when I was growing up. I thought they were beautiful. For several years I wanted to be a nun. I saw them as really pure, disciplined, above average people. They had these serene faces. Nuns are sexy.

Madonna

The one certain way for a woman to hold a man is to leave him for religion.

Muriel Spark, novelist.

God has no religion.
Mahatma Gandhi

I do benefits for all religions - I'd hate to blow the hereafter on a technicality.
Bob Hope, comedian.

God is for men and religion for women.
Joseph Conrad, novelist.

Adult baptisms increased dramatically following the installation of the font wave machine.

Puritanism, the haunting fear that someone, somewhere, may be happy.

H.L. Mencken

It is a great mistake to think that God is chiefly interested in religion.

William Temple

I've always known that Catholicism is a completely sexist, repressed, sin-and-punishment-based religion. I've already fallen out of love with Catholicism.

Madonna

Religion is caught not taught.

William Inge, Dean of St Paul's Cathedral.

One cannot be a Catholic and grown up.

George Orwell

It is no accident that the symbol of a bishop is a crook and the sign of an archbishop is a double-cross.

Dom Gregory Dix, British monk.

What church I go to on Sunday, what dogma of the Catholic Church I believe in, is my business, and whatever faith any other American has, is his business.

John F. Kennedy, US President.

After coming into contact with a religious man I always feel that I must wash my hands.

Friedrich Wilhelm Nietzsche

When the white man came we had the land and they had the Bibles; now they have the land and we have the Bibles.

Dan George, Canadian Indian chief.

I'm not really a practising Jew but I keep a kosher kitchen just to spite Hitler.

Miriam Margolyes, actress.

We must respect the other fellow's religion but only in the sense and to the extent that we respect his theory that his wife is beautiful and his children smart.

H.L. Mencken

As a Roman Catholic I thank God for the heretics. Heresy is only another word for freedom of thought.

Graham Greene, novelist.

MEN NEVER DO EVIL SO COMPLETELY AND CHEERFULLY AS WHEN THEY DO IT FROM RELIGIOUS CONVICTIONS.

Blaise Pascal

I am a Millionaire. That is my religion.

George Bernard Shaw

Once you're a Catholic, you're always a Catholic - in terms of your feelings of guilt and remorse and whether you've sinned or not. Sometimes I'm racked with guilt when I needn't be and that, to me, is left over from my Catholic upbringing. Because in Catholicism you are a born sinner and you are a sinner all your life. No matter how you try to get away with it, the sin is within you all the time.

Madonna

Religion is by no means a proper subject of conversation in a mixed company.

Eighteenth century, Earl of Chesterfield.

Many religious people are deeply suspicious. They seem - for purely religious purposes, of course - to know more about iniquity than the unregenerate.

Rudyard Kipling, novelist and poet.

She believed in nothing: only her scepticism kept her from being an atheist.

Jean-Paul Sartre

Catholicism is not a soothing religion. It's a painful religion. We're all gluttons for punishment.

Madonna

White is the virginal colour, symbolising purity and innocence. Why do nuns wear black?

Dave Allen, comedian.

At the present time the Anglican clergy wear their collars the wrong way round. I would compel them to wear, not only their collars, but all their clothes back to front.

Aldous Huxley, writer.

St Mark's Church members had doubled since the Spirit had come.

She was an atheist and I was an agnostic. We didn't know what religion *not* to bring our children up in.

Woody Allen

6: MONEY

A city bullion broker decided to adorn his notepaper with a suitable motto and asked staff for suggestions. The best they came up with was **Ingot We Trust.**

'The Times' Newspaper.

Money is like muck, not good except it be s p r e a d.

Francis Bacon, English philosopher.

Gain all you can, save all you can, give all you can.

Margaret Thatcher quoting John Wesley.

I don't need any bodyguards, but what I do need are a couple of expertly trained accountants.

Elvis Presley, singer.

Rich bachelors should be heavily taxed. It's not fair that some men should be happier than others.

Oscar Wilde

Keep your lives free from the l♥ve of money and be content with what you have.

Hebrews 13:5 (NIV)

Dallas. They call it the buckle on the Bible Belt. It has the largest number of millionaires, the worst crime rate and one of the severest poverty rates of any American city. Yet Dallas could also be described as the most Christian place on the earth. It has the highest proportion of paid-up church members in any city anywhere. And the majority embrace the most conservative form of Christianity.

Anthony Thomas, broadcaster.

Money it turned out, was exactly like $ex, you thought of nothing el$e if you didn't have it and thought of other thing$ if you did.

James Baldwin, writer.

No-one would have remembered the Good Samaritan if he had only had good intentions. He had money as well.

Margaret Thatcher

If all the economists were laid end to end they still wouldn't reach a conclusion.

George Bernard Shaw

Why does this workman ascend the highest scaffolding and risk his life, if you do not pay him his wages as soon as they are due?
The Talmud

I have enough money to last me the rest of my life, unless I buy something.
Jackie Mason, comedian.

I have a strange affinity with money. I make it and spend it.
Cher

Money is the poor man's credit card.
Marshall McLuhan, writer.

If you can actually count your money you are not a rich man.

John Paul Getty, rich man.

A lot of middle class people assume that working class people disapprove of wealth, but what they really disapprove of is their lack of it.

Ken Livingstone, British Member of Parliament.

Money brings some happiness, but after a certain point it just brings more money.

Neil Simon, singer.

True, you can't take it with you, but then that's not the place where it comes in handy.

Brendan Francis, writer.

He who loves money never has money enough, he who loves wealth never has enough profit; this too is vanity.

Ecclesiastes 5:9 (J.B. Phillips)

If Allah gives you prosperity he will give you the brains to go with it.

Turkish proverb

Money can't buy friends, but you can get a better class of enemy.

Spike Milligan

I never took pleasure in earning money. Money is not necessarily related to happiness. Maybe it is related to unhappiness.

John Paul Getty

Money's not important. I never think I want to make millions and millions of dollars but I don't want to have to worry about it. The more money you have the more problems you have. I went from making no money to making comparatively a lot and all I've had is problems. Life was simpler when I had no money, when I just barely survived.

Madonna

BUT godliness with contentment is great gain. For we brought nothing into the world and we can take nothing out of it. But if we have food and clothing, we will be content with that. People who want to get rich fall into temptation and a trap and into many foolish and harmful desires that plunge them into ruin and destruction. For the love of money is a root of all kinds of evil.

Paul's first letter to Timothy (6:6ff)

My mo$t £ervent hope i$ that I'll meet a man who love$ me £or my$el£ and not £or my money.

Christina Onassis, heiress.

Feel for others, in your pocket.

C.H. Spurgeon, preacher.

Money is like fertilizer. You have to spread it around everywhere, if not it stinks.

John Paul Getty

It is a kind of spiritual snobbery that makes people think they can be happy without money.

Albert Camus

Pennies do not come from heaven, they have to be earned here on earth.

Margaret Thatcher

O lord, thou knowest I have nine houses in the City of London and have lately purchased an estate in Essex. I beseech thee to preserve the counties of Middlesex and Essex from fires and earthquakes.
Joshua Ward

It's fine to make money. It isn't fine to make money your God.
< Sinead O'Connor

Do not lay up for yourselves treasures on earth, where moth and rust consume and where thieves break in and steal.
Matthew 6:19 (RSV)

I think whoever said money can't buy happiness simply hadn't found out where to go shopping.

Bo Derek, actress.

The world does not say, Blessed are the poor.

The world says, Blessed are the rich. You are worth as much as you have.

But Christ says, Wrong, Blessed are the poor, for theirs is the kingdom of heaven, because they do not put their trust in what is so transitory.

Oscar Romero

There's no reason to be the richest man in the cemetery.
You can't do any business there.

Colonel Sanders, US businessman.

I'd like to live like a poor man, but with a lot of money.

Pablo Picasso

Prosperity has often been fatal to Christianity, but persecution never.

An Amish leader quoted in 'The Economist'

"Do you really think I'm a material girl? I'm not. Take it, I don't need money I need love."

Madonna

I must say I hate money but it's the lack of it I hate most.

Katherine Mansfield, novelist.

THEN the Pharisees went out and laid plans to trap Jesus in his words. They sent their disciples to him along with the Herodians. "Teacher," they said, "We know you are a man of integrity and that you teach the way of God in accordance with the truth. You aren't swayed by men, because you pay no attention to who they are. Tell us then, what is your opinion? Is it right to pay taxes to Caesar or not?"

But Jesus, knowing their evil intent, said, "You hypocrites, why are you trying to trap me? Show me the coin used for paying the tax." They brought him a denarius, and he asked them, "Whose portrait is this? And whose inscription?"

"Caesar's," they replied.

Then he said to them, "Give to Caesar what is Caesar's, and to God what is God's."

When they heard this, they were amazed. So they left him and went away.

Matthew 22:15ff (NIV)

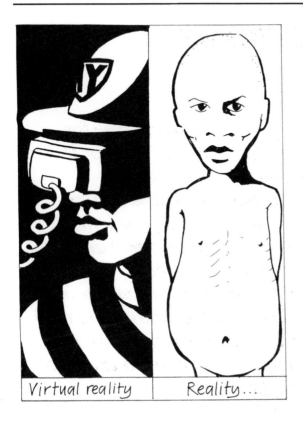

Virtual reality | Reality...

The meek shall inherit the earth, but not the mineral rights.

John Paul Getty

7: THE GOOD BOOK

The truth is that the light which shines in this incredible book simply cannot be put out.

Malcolm Muggeridge

The Bible is very like the poor: we have it always with us but we know very little about it.

Samuel Butler

THE Ten Commandments don't tell you what you ought to do. They just put ideas into your head.

Anon.

I can, just, come to imagine for myself that a man of more or less my own biological and social composition could have written Hamlet or Lear and gone home to lunch and found a normal answer to the question, 'How did it go today?' I cannot conceive of the author of the Speech Out of the Whirlwind in Job writing or dictating that text and dwelling within common existence and parlance.

George Steiner, journalist.

The number one book of the ages was written by a committee and it was called The Bible.

Louis B. Mayer, Hollywood film director.

I am puzzled about which Bible people are reading when they suggest religion and politics don't mix.

Desmond Tutu, South African archbishop.

If you believe what you like and reject what you like, it is not the Gospel you believe but yourself.

St Augustine

Mr Ron Burke wrote to the Newbury Weekly News concerning a sub-editor's alterations to a Christian Viewpoint article that he had written: "I realise that the translation of religious documents is open to interpretation, but when I said the Good Samaritan was "moved to get off his ass" I feel it translates better using the word "donkey" rather than your choice of "backside".

During a survey expedition I visited the island of Tristan da Cunha. The islanders were delighted with the gifts brought by the expeditions - except the Bibles. During the course of the years so many Bibles had been sent to the island that there was now an average of seven copies per inhabitant.

Francis K. Pearse, writer.

Say what you will about the Ten Commandments, you always come back to the pleasant fact that there are only ten of them.

H.L. Mencken

As the rain and the snow come down from heaven, and do not return to it without watering the earth and making it bud and flourish, so that it yields seed for the sower and bread for the eater, so is my word that goes out from my mouth: It will not return to me empty, but will accomplish what I desire and achieve the purpose for which I sent it.

Isaiah 55:10ff (NIV)

The God of the Bible is the God of liberation rather than oppression; a God of justice rather than injustice; a God of freedom and humanity rather than enslavement and subservience; a God of love, righteousness and community rather than hatred, self-interest and exploitation.

Allan Boesak, minister.

A man can't always be defending the truth. There must be a time to feed on it.

C.S. Lewis

More heated discussion of the holy scriptures.

The King James Version was completed on William Shakespeare's forty-sixth birthday. The forty-sixth word from the beginning of the King James translation of Psalm 46 is 'shake'.

It is written, ❛*Man does not live on bread alone, but on every word that comes from the mouth of God.*❜

Jesus in Matthew 4:4

I have sometimes seen more in a line of the Bible than I could well tell how to stand under, yet at another time the whole Bible hath been to me as dry as a stick.

John Bunyan, religious writer.

'You gentiles have taken everything from us', argued the Jew.

'Like what?' said the Christian.

'Like the Ten Commandments, for a start.'

'We may have taken them,' replied the Christian,

'But you can't possibly accuse us of keeping them!'

'Those who talk of the Bible as a "monument of English prose" are merely admiring it as a monument over the grave of Christianity.'
T.S. Eliot

When a preacher leaving Glamis Castle promised to send the Princess Elizabeth, then a little girl of ten, a book, she thanked him but asked if it could be, "Not about God. I know everything about him."
Robert Lacey, royal biographer.

In some respects my theology, like any theology, is heresy, if by heresy we mean a presentation of God's message that is incomplete, inadequate, and potentially dangerous... Anyone who endeavours to theologize for the people of his culture is guilty of missing an important dimension of the whole truth of God.
Tony Campolo, preacher.

A minister in Denver Colorado barbecue grilled a copy of the Good News Bible recently because he believes it misinterprets Scripture and is **"more insulting than pornography"**.

The minister describes himself as a *'primitive Christian'* and gave away copies of the traditional King James Bible to people attending the burning. He used a barbecue grill because the city prohibited open burning. **"I blame it on Satan who wants to sidetrack people by changing what they read."**

The new fundamentalists are very, very dangerous. To quote a preacher, "I had a sneak look at the back of the book" so I know that the good guys will win in the end. In the meantime, the bad guys are in control and religion has become an industry - something that has more in common with MacDonalds than it does with me.

Bono >

I want to see a new translation of the Bible into the hearts and conduct of living men and women. I want an improved translation - or transference it might be called - of the commandments and promises and teachings and influences of the Book to the minds and feelings and words and activities of the men and women who hold onto it and swear by it and declare it to be an inspired book and the only authorized rule of life.

T hat seems to me to be the only translation, after all, that will in the long run prove to be of any value...It is of no use making correct translations of words, if we cannot get the words translated into life.

William Booth, founder of The Salvation Army.

For the word of God is living and active. Sharper than any double-edged sword, it penetrates even to dividing soul and spirit, joints and marrow; it judges the thoughts and attitudes of the heart.

Hebrews 4:12 (NIV)

What we could do with is a special edition of the Bible - with the answers included, upside down at the back.

Peter Williams, writer.

8: THE GOOD NEWS - JESUS CHRIST ALMIGHTY

He whom the world could not inwrap
Yonder lies in Mary's lap.

Martin Luther

He himself bore our sins in his body on the tree, that we might die to sin and live for righteousness.

1 Peter 2:24 (NIV)

All historians must confess that the turning point of the race is the cross of Christ. It would be impossible to fix any other hinge of history. From that moment the power of evil received its mortal wound. It dies hard, but from that moment it was doomed.

Charles H. Spurgeon

GOD: WHAT THE CRITICS SAY

He was born in an obscure village, the child of a peasant woman.

He grew up in still another village, where he worked in a carpenter's shop until he was thirty. Then for three years he was an itinerant preacher.

He never wrote a book. He never had an office. He never had a family or owned a house. He didn't go to college. He never visited a big city. He never travelled two hundred miles from the place where he was born. He did none of the things one usually associated with greatness.

He had no credentials but himself.

He was only thirty-three when the tide of public opinion turned against him. His friends ran away. He was turned over to his enemies and went through the mockery of a trial. He was nailed to a cross between two thieves. While he was dying, his executioners gambled for his clothing, the only property he had on earth. When he was dead, he was laid in a borrowed grave through the pity of a friend.

Nineteen centuries have come and gone, and today he remains the central figure of the human race and the leader of mankind's progress. All the armies that ever marched, all the navies that ever sailed, all parliaments that ever sat, all the kings that ever reigned, put together, have not affected the life of man on this planet so much as that one solitary life.

Anon.

I WOULD OFTEN GET LETTERS SAYING IF CHRIST WERE HERE HE WOULD DO WHAT I WAS DOING; THEY SAW ME AS A CHRIST-LIKE AGENT BECAUSE HE SAID, CLOTHE THE NAKED, FEED THE POOR. I COULD DENY IT UNTIL I WAS BLUE IN THE FACE BUT THAT'S WHAT THEY WERE SAYING. MY POINT OF VIEW WAS THAT I'D SEEN THE WORST HORRORS BUT THEY WERE MAN-INDUCED AND THEREFORE MAN-SOLUBLE, THAT'S ALL. BUT I GOT EVERYTHING FROM CHRIST TO THE MOST OFF-BEAT KHARMIC PHILOSOPHY ATTRIBUTED TO ME.

Bob Geldof, pop singer and organiser of Live Aid for African famine relief.

When I was growing up I was religious in a passionate way. Jesus Christ was like a movie star, my favourite idol of all.

Madonna >

GOD: WHAT THE CRITICS SAY

I'm a real believer in Jesus. He was a great communicator of what later became socialist ideals. Take the story of the Good Samaritan; it just doesn't stop there. It's the beginning of welfare socialism. For that reason I can often see what Jesus was getting at much easier than I can wrap my mind around Marx and Engels. He was such a human person.

Billy Bragg, singer.

An electricity worker in Guyana, Ray Charles, who was convicted of assaulting a colleague in a scuffle, was given the option of singing a hymn or facing some other kind of punishment. A magistrate in Georgetown, K. Juman-Yasin, told Charles that he ought to have some singing talent because he had the same name as the American rhythm and blues singer. The 26-year-old then gave an off-key rendition of In The Name of Jesus, We Have the Victory. After a standing ovation from spectators he gave an encore and the magistrate discharged him with a reprimand.

*T*HE only real Jesus is one who is larger than life, who escapes our categories, who eludes our attempts to reduce him to manageable proportions so that we can claim him for our cause. Any Jesus who has been made to fit our formula ceases to be appealing precisely because he is no longer wondrous, mysterious, surprising. We may reduce him to right-wing Republican conservative or a gun-toting Marxist revolutionary and thus rationalize and justify our own political ideology. But having done so, we are dismayed to discover that whoever we have signed on as an ally is not Jesus. Categorize Jesus and he isn't Jesus anymore.

Andrew Greeley, novelist.

I may, I suppose, regard myself or pass for being a relatively successful man. People occasionally stare at me in the streets, that's fame. I can fairly easily earn enough to qualify for admission to the higher slopes of the Internal Revenue, that's success. Furnished with money and a little fame even the elderly, if they care to, may partake of trendy diversions, that's pleasure. It might happen once in a while that something I said or wrote was sufficiently heeded for me to persuade myself that it represented a serious impact on our time, that's fulfilment. Yet I say to you, and I beg you to believe me, multiply these tiny triumphs by a million, add them all together and they are nothing, less than nothing, a positive impediment, measured against one draught of that living water Christ offers to the spiritually thirsty, irrespective of who or what they are.

Malcolm Muggeridge

Another hellfire + brimstone sermon.

One of the awful things about writing when you are a Christian is that for you the ultimate reality is the Incarnation, the present reality is the Incarnation, and nobody believes in the Incarnation; that is, nobody in your audience. My audience are the people who think God is dead. At least these are the people I am conscious of writing for.

Flannery O'Connor, novelist.

Christ might be described as an under-privileged, colonial, working-class victim of political and religious persecution.

Prince Philip, Duke of Edinburgh.

Jesus came to raise the dead. The only qualification for the gift of the Gospel is to be dead.

You don't have to be smart.

You don't have to be good.

You don't have to be wise.

You don't have to be wonderful.

You don't have to be anything...

you just have to be dead. That's it.

Robert Farrar Capon, writer.

The whole religious complexion of the modern world is due to the absence from Jerusalem of a lunatic asylum.

Havelock Ellis, writer.

Christ beats his drum but he does not press men; Christ is served with voluntaries.

John Donne, poet.

He is despised and rejected of men; a man of sorrows and acquainted with grief: and we hid as it were our faces from him; he was despised and we esteemed him not.

Surely he hath borne our griefs and carried our sorrows: yet we did esteem him stricken, smitten of God, and afflicted.

But he was wounded for our transgressions, he was bruised for our iniquities: the chastisement of our peace was upon him; and with his stripes we are healed.

All we like sheep have gone astray; we have turned every one to his own way; and the Lord hath laid on him the iniquity of us all.

He was oppressed and he was afflicted, yet he opened not his mouth: he is brought as a lamb to the slaughter and as a sheep before her shearers is dumb so he did not open his mouth.

He was taken from prison and from judgment and who shall declare his generation? For he was cut off out of the land of the living: for the transgression of my people was he stricken.

And he made his grave with the wicked and with the rich in his death; because he had done no violence, neither was any deceit in his mouth.

Isaiah 53:3ff

We're more popular than Jesus.

< John Lennon of The Beatles.

We must not seek the child Jesus in the pretty figures of our Christmas cribs. We must seek him among the undernourished children who have gone to bed tonight without eating, among the poor newsboys who will sleep covered with newspapers in doorways.

Oscar Romero

Jesus was a typical man, they always say they'll come back but you never see them again.
Graffiti

Crucifixes are sexy because there's a naked man on them.

Madonna

If Christ had been as successful as Billy Graham, we should never have heard of him.
Malcolm Muggeridge

I SIMPLY ARGUE that the Cross be raised again at the centre of the market place as well as on the steeple of the church. I am recovering the claim that Jesus was not crucified in a cathedral between two candles, but on a cross between two thieves; on the town garbage heap; at a crossroad so cosmopolitan that they had to write His title in Hebrew and in Latin and in Greek (or shall we say in English, in Bantu and in Africaans?); at the kind of place where cynics talk smut and thieves curse and soldiers gamble. Because that is where He died. And that is what He died about. And that is where churchmen should be and what churchmanship should be about.

George MacLeod, founder of the Iona Community.

I've met people who have been on hard drugs who were saved through fundamentalist religion, were saved by Jesus. They really were. That's a starting point. I guess it depends on what people's needs are. I never felt a need for that sort of concreteness. Maybe I'm lucky. Me, I like it wide open.

Bruce Springsteen

King Christ the world is all aleak; and life preservers there are none.

E.E. Cummings, poet.

You see, at just the right time, when we were still powerless, Christ died for the ungodly. Very rarely will anyone die for a righteous man, though for a good man someone might possibly dare to die. But God demonstrates his own love for us in this: While we were still sinners, Christ died for us.

Paul the Apostle in his letter to the Church at Rome (5:6ff, NIV)

If Jesus Christ were to come today, people would not crucify him. They would ask him to dinner and hear what he had to say and make fun of it.

Thomas Carlyle

Our society has taken Jesus and recreated him in our own cultural image. When I hear Jesus being proclaimed from the television stations across our country, from pulpits hither and yon, he comes across not as the biblical Jesus but as a white Anglo-Saxon, Protestant Republican. God created us in His image, but we have decided to return the favour and create a God who is in our image.

Tony Campolo

How else but through a
broken h♥art
May Lord Christ enter in?

Oscar Wilde

The arduous demands of aquarium management have taught me a deep appreciation for what is involved in running a universe based on dependable physical laws. To my fish I am deity, and one who does not hesitate to intervene...I often long for a way to communicate with those small-brained water dwellers. Out of ignorance, they perceive me as a constant threat. I cannot convince them of my true concern...To change their perceptions would require a form of incarnation.

Philip Yancey, journalist.

'If I had been the Virgin Mary I would have said no'

STEVIE SMITH

If a man came up to me and said he was Jesus Christ, I'd point him to the bargain basement. It's the 20th century and you can't walk around in those shoes he used to wear. I'd tell him he's in the wrong supermarket. Safeways is better value. On a more serious level I'd say that if Jesus Christ were on earth you'd find him in a gay bar in San Francisco. He'd be working with people suffering from AIDS. These people are the new lepers. Just like the turn of BC/AD. Don't touch them, walk away from them. If you want to find out where Jesus would be hanging out, it'll always be with the lepers.

Bono

A boy threw a stone at the stained glass window of the Incarnation. It nicked out the 'E' in the word HIGHEST in the text, 'GLORY TO GOD IN THE HIGHEST'. Thus, till unfortunately it was mended, it read, 'GLORY TO GOD IN THE HIGH ST.'

George MacLeod

Come unto me, all ye that labour and are heavy laden, and I will give you rest.

Jesus, Matthew 11:28 (AV)

Lloyd Douglas's most important decision in his book *The Robe* was not to permit Jesus on stage. We learn about Him through the memories and experiences of those who did know Him...The Lord, not to put too fine an edge on things, is a slippery one. He can be captured, more or less, by the visual arts because they do not require that He speak or move or act. But in the literary arts He appears either too good to be human or too human to be good. Sometimes, as in the case of *Jesus Christ Superstar*, the author manages both errors. Douglas, by keeping Jesus offstage, preserves that which is essential in Jesus: His elusiveness, His disconcerting refusal to fit into any of the categories with which we attempt to contain Him.

Andrew Greeley

*H*E is the image of the invisible God, the firstborn over all creation. For by him all things were created: things in heaven and on earth, visible and invisible, whether thrones or powers or rulers or authorities; all things were created by him and for him. He is before all things, and in him all things hold together. And he is the head of the body, the church; he is the beginning and the firstborn from among the dead, so that in everything he might have supremacy. For God was pleased to have all his fulness dwell in him, and through him to reconcile to himself all things, whether things on earth or things in heaven, by making peace through his blood, shed on the cross.

Paul's letter to the Church at Colossae (1:15ff, NIV)

if

Jesus were born one thousand times in Bethlehem and not in me, then I would still be lost.

Corrie ten Boom, anti-Nazi Christian activist.

Mary and Joseph approach the innkeeper who tells them there is no room in the inn.
Joseph: *But my wife is pregnant.*
Innkeeper: *Well, it's not my fault.*
Joseph: *It's not my fault either!*

A children's nativity play.

Enid stopped at nothing in her attempts to spread the good news.

You're worried about permissiveness - about the way the preaching of grace seems to say it's okay to do all kinds of terrible things as long as you just walk in afterward and take the free gift of God's forgiveness...

While you and I may be worried about seeming to give permission, Jesus apparently wasn't. He wasn't afraid of giving the prodigal son a kiss instead of a lecture, a party instead of probation; and he proved that by bringing in the elder brother at the end of the story and having him raise much the same objections you do. He's angry about the party. He complains that his father is lowering the standards and ignoring virtue - that music, dancing and a fatted calf are, in effect, just so many permissions to break the law.

And to that, Jesus has the father say only one thing: 'Cut that out! We're not playing good boys and bad boys anymore. Your brother was dead and he's alive again. The name of the game from now on is resurrection, not bookkeeping.'

Robert Farrar Capon, writer.

I met this guy once in a mental hospital I was visiting. He introduced himself to me as Jesus Christ. I just said, 'Haven't we met before?' He said nothing. I asked him why, if he was the Son of God, was he in a mental hospital? He said, 'Because it's my 40 days and 40 nights in the wilderness.' At that point I just cracked up. I asked him when the end of the world was going to come. He said April 1st. I thought, 'Brilliant, pencil it into the diary. The world will end on April Fool's Day. Perfect.'

Bono

When Christ appeared in Zebulun and Naphtali
curing the sick
raising the dead
preaching to the poor
bringing hope to the peoples,
something began on earth like when a stone
is cast into a quiet lake and starts ripples
that finally reach the furthest shores
Christ appeared in Zebulun and Naphtali
with the signs of liberation:
shaking off oppressive yokes
bringing joy to hearts
sowing hope
And this is what God is doing now in history.

Oscar Romero

9: THE BAD NEWS - PAIN AND SUFFERING

Yet man is born unto trouble, as the sparks fly upwards.

Job 5:7 (AV)

ONLY TWO GROUPS OF SPECIES KILL MEMBERS OF THE SAME SPECIES WHOLESALE, RATS AND MEN.

C.S. Lewis

It would be just another illusion to believe that reaching out to God will free us from pain and suffering. Often, indeed, it will take us where we would rather not go. But we know that without going there we will not find our life.

Henri Nouwen

Anywhere I see suffering, that is where I want to be, doing what I can.

Princess Diana, the Princess of Wales, talking to a man with AIDS.

I read the Book of Job last night: I don't think God comes well out of it.

Virginia Woolf

I don't envy those who have never known any pain, physical or spiritual, because I strongly suspect that the capacity for pain and the capacity for joy are equal. Only those who have suffered great pain are able to know equally great joy.

Madeleine L'Engle, writer.

A man may perform astonishing feats and comprehend a vast amount of knowledge and yet have no understanding of himself. But suffering directs a man to look within. If it succeeds, then there, within him, is the beginning of his learning.

Søren Kierkegaard

For my life is spent with grief, and my years with sighing: my strength faileth because of mine iniquity, and my bones are consumed.

Psalm 31:10 (AV)

Nothing worth having comes without some kind of fight Got to kick at the darkness till it bleeds daylight.

< *Bruce Cockburn*

If our God were a pagan god or the god of intellectuals He might fly to His remotest heaven and our grief would force him down to earth again. But you know that our God came to be among us. Shake your fist at Him, spit in His face, scourge Him and finally crucify Him: what does it matter...? It's already been done to him.

George Bernanos, writer.

117

I don't know what will happen now, we've got some difficult days ahead. It really doesn't matter with me now, because I've been on the mountain top. I won't mind. Like anybody I would like to live a long life. Longevity has its place. But I'm not concerned about that just now. I want to do God's will and he's allowed me to go up to the mountain, and I've looked over and I've seen the Promised Land. I may not get there with you, but I want you to know that we as a people will get to the Promised Land. Well, I'm happy tonight. I'm not fearing any man. Mine eyes have seen the glory of the coming of the Lord.

Martin Luther King

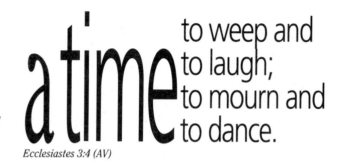

a time to weep and to laugh; to mourn and to dance.

Ecclesiastes 3:4 (AV)

Every night I still ask the Lord *'why'* and I still haven't heard a decent answer yet.

Jack Kerouac, writer.

I have lost my daughter and we shall miss her. But I bear no ill will, I bear no grudge. Dirty sort of talk is not going to bring her back to life. Don't ask me, please, for a purpose. I don't have a purpose. I don't have an answer. But I know there has to be a plan. If I didn't think that I would commit suicide. It's part of a greater plan and God is good. And we shall meet again.

Gordon Wilson, whose daughter Marie was killed by a terrorist bomb at Enniskillen in Northern Ireland.

Despair has been called the unforgivable sin - not presumably because God refuses to forgive it but because it despairs of the possibility of being forgiven.

Frederich Buechner

GOD comforts us in all our troubles, so that we can comfort those in any trouble with the comfort we ourselves have received.

Paul's second letter to the Church at Corinth (2 Cor 1:4, NIV)

Forgive your enemies
but never forget
their names.

John F. Kennedy

All have sinned
and fall short of
the glory of God.

Paul's letter to the Church at Rome (3:23, NIV)

Right is right
even if nobody
does it.
Wrong is wrong
even if
everybody is
wrong about it.

G.K. Chesterton

I hate to advocate drugs, alcohol, violence or insanity to anyone, but they've always worked for me.

Hunter S. Thompson, writer

The Christian faith is the most exciting drama that ever staggered the imagination of man - and the dogma is the drama. The plot pivots upon a single character, and the whole action is the answer to a single central problem: **what think ye of Christ?**

Dorothy L. Sayers, novelist.

Miserable man! A toad is a bog of poison and a spider a blister of poison and yet a toad and a spider cannot poison themselves; man hath a dram of poison, original sin, in an invisible corner, we know not where, and he cannot choose but poison himself and all his actions with that...

John Donne

Who in heart not ever kneels Neither sin nor Saviour feels.

George Herbert

As for you, you were dead in your transgressions and sins, in which you used to live when you followed the ways of this world and of the ruler of the kingdom of the air, the spirit who is now at work in those who are disobedient. All of us also lived among them at one time, gratifying the cravings of our sinful nature and following its desires and thoughts. Like the rest, we were by nature objects of wrath.

Paul's letter to the Christians at Ephesus (2:1-3, NIV)

I FELT MORE CONTENT WITH MYSELF. YOU KNOW IT BECOMES AN ENORMOUS RELIEF TO KNOW THERE IS SOMETHING THERE, A LOVELY FEELING. I DON'T KNOW WHAT I DID, IT JUST CAME, JUST BRILLIANT...BUT IT'S HOW I FELT AND HOW I FEEL NOW; COMING TO FAITH HAS BEEN SO MARVELLOUS.

Maire Ni Bhraonian, singer, Clannad.

We're all sinners. People seem to think that because their sins are different from other people's sins, they're not sinners. People don't like to think of themselves as sinners. It makes them feel uncomfortable.

Bob Dylan, singer. >

Virtue has its own rewards, but no sales at the box office.

Mae West

There are words that I have never quite understood, such as sin.

Albert Camus

We didn't invent sin. We're just trying to improve it.

Graffiti

At some point you have to take account of your own actions. We can't keep on saying the problems is capitalism or communism or poverty or ecology. Of course these things have to be dealt with, but we have to stop blaming The Other and look inside.

Roland Orzabal, singer, Tears for Fears.

You always get the Bible thumping brigade. The fact that I'm earning money from the misdeeds of my past must really get up their noses something terrible but I'm perfectly convinced that the majority of clear-thinking people in England would be in favour of my being pardoned.

Ronnie Biggs, escaped Great Train Robber, living in Brazil.

Death is life's answer to 'Why?'.

Graffiti

This is a faithful saying and worthy of all acceptation, that Christ Jesus came into the world to save sinners; of whom I am chief.

1 Tim1:15 (AV)

We have met the enemy - and he is in us.

Don Henley, singer.

No man can break any of the ten commandments, he can only break himself against them.

G.K. Chesterton

Wickedness is a myth invented by good people to account for the curious attractiveness of others.

Oscar Wilde

The major sin is the sin of being born.

Samuel Beckett, novelist and playwright.

He who passively accepts evil is as much involved in it as he who helps to perpetrate it.

He who accepts evil without protesting against it is really co-operating with it.

Martin Luther King

Peradventure some sinner will say, 'perceive nor feel any weight in myself, do I ever so many sins.' To whom we answer that if a dog having a great stone bound about his neck is cast down from a high tower, he feels no weight of that stone as long as he is falling down, but when he is once fallen to the ground he is burst all to pieces by the reason of that stone.

John Fisher, Bishop of Rochester, (c.1508).

I know you're obeying your conscience but couldn't you do it a bit differently so as not to annoy people?

Anton Chekhov, writer.

All of a sudden this heavy weight that had been suppressing me for years finally lifted. I felt like somebody took tons off me. The anger and oppression of a diseased spirit was gone. I felt like a new person and like my whole life was ahead of me. I didn't feel that empty, sick feeling any more. I felt that God gave me a reason to be here.

< Donna Summer, singer.

I can truthfully say that I am slow to see the blemishes of fellow beings, being myself full of them. And, therefore, being in need of their charity, I have learnt not to judge anyone harshly and to make allowances for defects that I may detect.

Mahatma Gandhi

t he Lord is my light and my salvation; whom shall I fear? he Lord is the strength of my life; of whom shall I be afraid?

Psalm 27:1(AV)

THE most difficult thing in my life is to admit lust, anger and hatred. But when I talk with God I can't say simply and vaguely, 'Forgive me all of my sins'. I must spell them out and that hurts. So I tell him I was lusting after someone else or grasping for advantage or derogating an opponent. And then belief in the forgiveness of God gives me a deep security, confidence and independence of everyday concerns.

Jimmy Carter

Men struck down by affliction are at the foot of the Cross, almost at the greatest possible distance from God. It must not be thought that sin is a greater distance, it is a turning of our gaze in the wrong direction.

Simone Weil, philosopher.

All the seven deadly sins are self-destroying, morbid appetites, but in their early stages at least, lust and gluttony, avarice and sloth know some gratification, while anger and pride have power, even though that power eventually destroys itself. Envy is impotent, numbed with fear, never ceasing in its appetite, and it knows no gratification but endless self-torment. It has the ugliness of a trapped rat, which gnaws its foot in an effort to escape.

Angus Wilson, writer.

Between two evils, I always pick the one I never tried before.

Mae West

Adam was but human - this explains it all. He did not want the apple for the apple's sake, he wanted it only because it was forbidden. The mistake was in not forbidding the serpent; then he would have eaten the serpent.

Mark Twain

For whosoever shall call upon the name of the Lord shall be saved.

Paul's letter to the Church at Rome (10:13, AV)

The sinning is the best part of repentance.

Arabic proverb

'**Who then can be saved?**' **the disciples asked Jesus.**

Jesus looked straight at them and answered,

'*This is impossible for man but for God everything is possible.*'

Matthew 19:25-6

EVILDOING has a threshold magnitude. Yes, a human being hesitates and bobs back and forth between good and evil all his life. He slips, falls back, clambers up, repents, things begin to darken again. But just so long as the threshold of evildoing is not crossed, the possiblity of returning remains, and he himself is still within reach of our help. But when, through the density of evil actions, the result of either their own extreme degree or the absoluteness of his power, he suddenly crosses that threshold, he has left humanity behind and without, perhaps, the possibility of return.

Alexander Solzhenitsyn, writer.

When our Lord and Master called us to repent, he called us to a life of repentance.

Martin Luther

He who makes a beast of himself, gets rid of the pain of being a man.

Dr Johnson, writer.

I think we're all capable of becoming the worst, the child molester, the murderer, the thief. Not to admit it is to go mad. We must steer a middle course and say, 'Yes, I have this potential. But I also have the opposite potential, to be St Francis of Assisi.' We have Genghis Khan on one side and St Francis on the other and to steer a course between the two is sanity.

< *Sting, singer.*

11: PRAYER

Recent medical research in San Francisco suggests that the ways in which the Almighty moves may not always be mysterious. Two hundred patients admitted with heart attacks to the coronary care unit in San Francisco general hospital over a six-month period were allocated a group of Born Again Christians who said daily prayers on their behalf.

Another 200 patients acted as a control group and were subjected to a regime devoid of divine intercession. For them, evangelical helpmates joined the lists of things coronary victims are not supposed to have, like strong drink, strenous sexual activity or quarter pound hamburgers.

Dr Randolph Byrd, who organised the study, reported that significantly fewer patients being prayed for required ventilation, diuretics or antibiotics and fewer were classified as having a bad outcome, cardiac arrest, stroke, further heart attack, while in hospital, or death. 'Intercessory prayer has a beneficial therapeutic effect,' he said.

Sceptics draw support from Francis Galton, the eminent Victorian scientist, who applied his mind to the proposition that prayers for the sick helped to effect a speedy recovery. He pointed out that no one had prayers for a long and healthy life said on their behalf more frequently than the royal family; he compiled a league table that showed that the life expectancy of its members was in fact below average.

'The Times' newspaper.

The prayer of someone righteous is powerful and effective.

James 5:16

A sixty two year old friend of mine went to bed at night and prayed, ❛Please God, give me a skin like a teenager's.❜ Next day she woke up with pimples.

Phyllis Diller, writer.

Prayer must never be answered: ✉ if it is, it ceases to be prayer and becomes ✎ correspondence.

Oscar Wilde

To clasp hands in prayer is the beginning of an uprising against the disorder of the world.

Karl Barth, theologian.

GOD: WHAT THE CRITICS SAY

Among the remembered prayers of the very wise and holy St Thomas More is this: 'The things, good Lord, that we pray for, give us the grace to labour for.' A good example of somebody who understood this is a little girl whom Leslie Weatherhead mentioned in one of his early books. She was much troubled by the fact that her older brother trapped rabbits, and she begged him in vain to stop. One night her mother heard her praying: 'Dear God, please stop Tommy from trapping rabbits. Please don't let them get trapped. They can't. They *won't*! Amen.' Her mother, troubled and perplexed, asked, 'Darling, how can you be so sure that God won't let the rabbits be trapped?' The blessed child calmly replied: 'Because I jumped on the traps and sprung them!' *Ex ore infantium.* When I tell this story in sermons I see smiles. It is a charming one - but not a cute one. It is a paradigm of Christian praying.

Carroll E. Simcox, minister.

Prayer changes things

I pray when I'm in trouble or when I'm happy. When I feel any sort of extreme. *I pray* when I feel so great that I think I need to check in with myself and recognise how good life is. I know that sounds silly, but when it seems there's so much junk around, it's important just to remind myself of the things I have to be grateful for. On the other hand, when I'm feeling really bad or sad, *I pray* to try to reassure myself. It's all a kind of rationalisation. I can't describe the way I pray. **It has nothing to do with religion.**

Madonna

Lord, make me an instrument of your peace
Where there is hatred, let me sow love,
Where there is injury, pardon
Where there is doubt, faith
Where there is despair, hope,
Where there is darkness, light
Where there is sadness, joy
O Divine Master, grant that I may not so much seek to be consoled as to console
not so much to be understood as to understand
not so much to be loved as to love
for it is in giving that we receive
it is pardoning that we are pardoned
it is in dying that we awake to eternal life

St Francis of Assisi

On transcontinental flights I would recite the Lord's Prayer to myself on take-off and landings. One day in May 1981 I found myself murmuring, ❛*Our Father, which art in Heaven, Hollywood by thy name,*❜ and realised it was time to get out.

Steven Bach, Hollywood film producer.

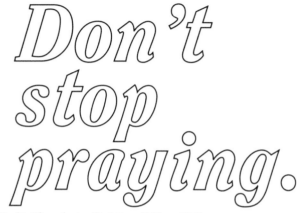

Paul to Thessalonian Christians (1 Thess. 5:17)

Please make the bad people good and the good people nice.

A child's prayer

I don't want to bore God.

Orson Welles, film director, explaining why he didn't pray.

Christians must remember that prayer is like the mortar that holds the bricks together, or the quiet pauses in a symphony. Without the mortar everything falls apart; without the quiet between the notes, no music. And without daily private prayer, Christians face spiritual anorexia.

Mitch Finley, minister.

Some people pray. Some people play guitar.

Bruce Springsteen

Real prayer is a serious concern, for we are speaking to the Sovereign Lord of all the universe, who is willing to move heaven and earth in answer to sincere and reasonable prayer. Prayer is not a mechanical duty, but a wonderful opportunity to develop a loving and caring relationship with the most important Person in our lives.

John Bunyan

Fighting the good fight

Prayer gives a man the opportunity of getting to know a gentleman he hardly ever meets. I do not mean his maker, but himself.
William Inge

The idea that He would take his attention away from the universe in order to give me a bicycle with three speeds is just so unlikely that I can't go along with it.
Quentin Crisp, writer.

Theologian as occupation holds no exalted place in my hierarchy of paying jobs. I am not a theologian for the same reason I am not a tractor mechanic - occupational choice.

Yet I am a tractor mechanic. Yesterday I took the distributor cap off the old machine I had left in the snow and dried the condenser. The tractor still wouldn't start but in that act I had become a mechanic. In the same fashion I have a neighbour, an electrician by occupation, who is a theologian. He told me he would not teach his child to pray, "Now I lay me down to sleep..." because, he said, the words could be a reminder to God to put her on His agenda that night. That is a theological statement because it is a statement about the kind of God God is. My neighbour is a 'little theologian' as Barth put it. And I am a little tractor mechanic.

Will Campbell, writer and minister.

From silly devotions and from sour-faced saints good Lord, deliver us.

St Teresa of Avila

Pray for the dead and fight like hell for the living.

Mother Jones, political activist.

Do not be anxious about anything, but in everything by prayer and petition, with thanksgiving, present your requests to God **And** the peace of God, which transcends all understanding, will guard your hearts and your minds in Christ Jesus.

Paul writing to the Philippian Church (4:6ff, NIV)

A curate, having taken considerable trouble to prepare a speech, found himself to his disgust, called upon only to lead the audience in prayer. Determined not to waste his material, he incorporated most of it in his prayer. One passage ran: **"** Lest this point be too obscure, O Lord, permit thy servant to illustrate it with an anecdote...**"**

Make me, dear Lord, polite and kind
To everyone I pray
And may I ask you how you find
Yourself, dear Lord, today?
A child's prayer

WHEN you pray, do not use a lot of meaningless words as the pagans do, who think that God will hear them because their prayers are long. Do not be like them. Your Father already knows what you need before you ask him.

PRAY like this, Our Father in Heaven, hallowed be your name, your kingdom come, your will be done on earth as it is in Heaven. Give us today our daily bread. Forgive us our debts, as we also have forgiven our debtors. And lead us not into temptation, but deliver us from the evil one.

Jesus (Matthew 6:7ff)

12: HEAVEN AND HELL, ANGELS AND DEVILS

The Devil is a Judaeo-Christian concept, the adversary of their God. Our gods don't have such adversaries. There is no active evil in the universe. Evil is what human beings do through lack of understanding. I've never met a Satanist in 20 years in the occult.

Vivianne Crowley, Secretary of The Pagan Association.

F OR *we wrestle not against flesh and blood, but against principalities, against powers, against the rulers of the darkness of this world, against spiritual wickedness in high places.*

Paul writing to the Ephesian Church (6:12, AV)

I do not believe in the Devil. The tendency of a number of religions, including Christianity to some extent, to have a quasi-independent centre of evil just adds to the mythological picture of things. It's an attempt to cope with the problem of evil which does not cope with it. Evil is a mystery but there are evil things we should take responsibility for.

David Jenkins, Bishop of Durham.

I don't know how much people think of Mick (Jagger) as the Devil or as just a good rock performer or what. There are black magicians who think we are acting as unknown agents of Lucifer and others who think we are Lucifer.

Keith Richard of The Rolling Stones, at the time of their recording of 'Sympathy for the Devil'.

The only ultimate disaster that can befall us is to feel ourselves to be at home here on earth. As long as we are aliens we cannot forget our true homeland which is that other kingdom You proclaimed.

Malcolm Muggeridge

I had far rather walk as I do in daily terror of eternity than feel that this was only a children's game in which all the contestants would get equally worthless prizes in the end.

T.S. Eliot

Where exactly _do_ angels fear to tread?

Everybody wants to go to Heaven but nobody wants to die.

Joe Louis, boxer.

I don't want to go to Heaven if you have to stand all the time.

Spike Milligan

_I_ _N my Father's house are many mansions: if it were not so, I would have told you. I go to prepare a place for you. And if I go and prepare a place for you, I will come again, and receive you unto myself; that where I am, there ye may be also._

Jesus in John 14:2-3 (AV)

If on the Judgement Day, I was confronted by God and I found that God took himself seriously, I would ask to go to the other place.

Malcolm Muggeridge

When we get to heaven we'll find American marines guarding the gate.

President Ronald Reagan

People are free in this world to live for themselves alone if they want to and let the rest go hang, and they are free to live out the dismal consequences as long as they can stand it. The doctrine of Hell proclaims that they retain this same freedom in whatever world comes next. Thus the possibility of making damned fools of ourselves would appear to be limitless.

Frederich Buechner

For a man in his wife's arms to be hankering after the other world is, in mild terms, a piece of bad taste, and not God's will. It's presumptuous to want to have everything at once - matrimonial bliss, the cross, and the heavenly Jerusalem, where they neither marry nor are given in marriage. Everything has its time.

Dietrich Bonhoeffer

THE CAREER OF JAMES DEAN HAS NOT ENDED. IT HAS JUST BEGUN. AND GOD HIMSELF IS DIRECTING THE PRODUCTION.

Pastor Xen Harvey at James Dean's funeral.

DEAREST JIMMY, ALL THIS REMEMBRANCE OF YOU ON YOUR ANNIVERSARY IS A WASTE OF TIME BECAUSE I KNOW YOU ARE STILL ALIVE. WHY WORRY SO MUCH ABOUT THE WAY YOU LOOK BECAUSE YOUR FANS WORSHIP YOU NO MATTER HOW DISFIGURED YOU ARE.

Fan letter to James Dean a year after his death in a motorcycle crash.

THE OLDER GENERATION HAD GOD. WE HAVE JAMES DEAN.

Anonymous teenage interviewee in 1957.

JAMES DEAN WORSHIPPED AND REACHED FOR IMMORTALITY. HE GOT WHAT HE WANTED.

Morrissey

Women give themselves to God when the devil wants nothing more to do with them.

Sophie Arnould, opera singer.

An apology for the Devil: it must be remembered that we have only heard one side of the case. God has written all the books.

Samuel Butler

Someone wrote in that we are God-haters. We get letters sent by anonymous religious maniacs who never put their address on and the last one said that we are all going to burn in a lake of fire. It's quite annoying.

Chris Donald, founder and editor of 'Viz' magazine.

A British research organisation calculated that the population of Heaven is 5,473,000,000. It reached the heavenly roll call tally by adding up all the deaths since 40,000BC - roughly 60 billion - then figuring out the world's Christian population and doing an estimate from 8,000BC.

ENTER through the narrow gate. For wide is the gate and broad is the road that leads to destruction and many enter through it.

BUT small is the gate and . narrow the road that leads to life, and only a few find it.

Jesus in Matthew 7:13 (NIV)

"No eye has seen, no ear has heard, no mind has conceived what God has prepared for those who love him."

The Apostle Paul quoting Isaiah in his first letter to the Church at Corinth (2:9, NIV)

If the devil doesn't exist but man has created him, he has created him in his own image and likeness.

Feodor Dostoevsky

We are very shy nowadays of even mentioning Heaven. We are afraid of the jeer about 'pie in the sky' and of being told that we are trying to 'escape from the duty of making a happy world here and now into dreams of a happy world elsewhere'. But either there is 'pie in the sky' or there is not. If there is not then Christianity is false for this doctrine is woven into its whole fabric. If there is, then this truth, like any other, must be faced, whether it is useful at political meetings or not.

C.S. Lewis

A church is a place in which gentlemen who have never been to Heaven brag about it to persons who will never get there.

H.L. Mencken

JEAN-
PAUL
SATRE

I believe in the Devil, first of the jins, created by God from fire, while man was made from clay. The Devil refused God's command to bow down to man and so God said, 'Out'. The Devil is the enemy of humankind; every single man and woman has a child of the Devil who tries to tempt him to disobey God.

Hesham El-Essawy, Islamic Society for the Promotion of Religious Tolerance.

God disarmed the principalities and powers and made a public spectacle of them, triumphing over them by the cross.

Paul to the Colossian Church (2:15)

I don't believe in the Devil but I do believe in the power of evil. I take the New Testament accounts of the Devil as being about that evil power. But in the end evil is personal because it affects one personally. I cannot believe in a man with horns or any of that stuff.

Lord Longford, politician.

The evidence for the Devil's existence is all around: our country going downhill, kids sleeping with each other, girls on the pill, horror videos, old people being raped, hooliganism. The Devil is behind it. Satanists believe we are at the beginning of the Reign of Satan, that the 1990s will see the unleashing of Satan's power, when all decency will disappear.

Audrey Harper, former Satanic high priestess turned Christian.

I do believe in the Devil and I'm very much against Halloween and all it stands for because it seems to be toying with something far too serious for a kids' game. By the Devil I do not mean a horned character with a tail, but if there is a personal God who is all good then I believe in a force for the opposite - a force for evil who is wholly bad.

Cliff Richard, singer.

People who believe they are going there often wonder what they will do with themselves in heaven. They make the mistake of assuming that the place will be all complete, finished to the last bit of gilding when they get there. But of course it won't.

J.B. Priestley, writer.

A PERSON (SATAN) WHO HAS DURING ALL TIME MAINTAINED THE IMPOSING POSITION OF SPIRITUAL HEAD OF FOUR-FIFTHS OF THE HUMAN RACE AND POLITICAL HEAD OF THE WHOLE OF IT, MUST BE GRANTED THE POSSESSION OF EXECUTIVE ABILITIES OF THE LOFTIEST ORDER.

Mark Twain

Modern man, if he dared to be articulate about his concept of heaven, would describe a vision which would look like the biggest department store in the world, showing new things and gadgets and himself having plenty of money with which to buy them.

Erich Fromm, psychologist.

Even Satan disguises himself as an angel of light.

Paul, in his second letter to the Corinthian Church (11:14).

*There is a dreadful Hell
And everlasting pains
There sinners must with devils dwell
In darkness, fire and chains.*

Isaac Watts, hymnwriter.

We **all** long for heaven where God is but we have it in our power to be in heaven with Him right now, to be happy with Him at this very moment. But being happy with Him now means:
loving as He loves
helping as He helps
giving as He gives
serving as He serves
rescuing as He rescues
being with Him for all the twenty-four hours
touching Him in His distressing disguise.

Mother Teresa of Calcutta.

Evil comes at leisure like the disease; good comes in a hurry like the doctor.

G.K. Chesterton

Let us ✳ ✦ ✱ ❖ ✘ swear while we may, for in Heaven it will not be allowed.

Mark Twain

Angels can fly because they take themselves lightly.

G.K. Chesterton

❛ *It may be the devil or it may be the Lord but you're gonna have to serve somebody.* **❜**

Bob Dylan

I think the resurrection of the body, unless much improved in construction, a mistake.

Evelyn Underhill, writer.

There is no reason why good cannot triumph as often as evil. The triumph of anything is a matter of organisation. If there are such things as angels I hope they are organised along the lines of the Mafia.

Kurt Vonnegut

Both Jerry Lee Lewis and Little Richard were Bible students. And Jerry Lee is the other famous example of the 'hellhound on your trail'. His line was, 'I'll take the left-hand path and I'll get to heaven by showing everybody what *not* to do.' Nice one! That's a good one baby! I'll drink to that!

Keith Richard >

This world cannot explain its own difficulties without the assistance of another.

Charles Caleb Colton, 1825.

Some want to live within the sound Of Church and chapel bell I want to run a rescue shop Within a yard of hell.

C.T. Studd, missionary and cricketer.

We may not pay Satan reverence, for that would be indiscreet, but we can at least respect his talents.

Mark Twain

Don't bother to think ahead. Tomorrow will soon be yesterday.

Graffiti

Hell has three gates: lust, anger and greed.

Bhagavadgita

One thing I shall miss in heaven is gardening. I don't know; we shan't have weeds in heaven, shall we?

Catherine Bramwell Booth, Salvationist.

If you go to Heaven without being naturally qualified for it you will not enjoy yourself there.

George Bernard Shaw

PEOPLE WHO DO THINK THEY ARE GOING THERE OFTEN WONDER WHAT THEY WILL DO WITH THEMSELVES IN HEAVEN.

J.B. Priestley

Believe in something for another world but don't be too set on what it is and then you won't start out that life with a disappointment.

Will Rogers

AND there was war in heaven. Michael and his angels fought against the dragon and the dragon and his angels fought back. But he was not strong enough, and they lost their place in heaven. The great dragon was hurled down - that ancient serpent called the devil, or Satan, who leads the whole world astray. He was hurled to earth, and all his angels with him.

Revelation 12:7ff (NIV)

AND the devil, who deceived them, was thrown into the lake of burning sulphur, where the beast and the false prophet had been thrown. They will be tormented day and night for ever and ever.

Revelation 20:10ff (NIV)

Eternity is a terrible thought. I mean, where's it going to end?

Tom Stoppard, playwright.

In that sweet by and by we shall meet on that beautiful shore.

Ira David Sankey, hymnwriter and preacher.

13: CHRISTIANS, CHRISTIANITY AND OTHER GOOD IDEAS

We're all bastards but God loves us anyway.

Will Campbell, asked to summarise Christianity in less than ten words.

I don't know which will go first: rock 'n' roll or Christianity.

John Lennon

I am convinced that often the world doesn't take Christians seriously because we are so much like the world; caught up in the same miserable rat race of self-seeking consumerism and materialism.

Tom Sine, writer.

Can you imagine how it feels to believe in Christ and be so uncomfortable with Christianity? The church is an empty, hollow building. It's the edifice. The established church is the edifice of Christianity. It's as if when the spirit of God leaves a place, the only things that are left are the pillars of rules and regulations to keep its roof on.

Bono

Christianity has survived Christians for two thousand years now, which from my point of view is evidence that maybe something is going on there.

T. Bone Burnett

I do believe in God. Yes, and more than I believe in God, I believe in the ideal of Christianity itself. If we could be true Christians, the whole world might be a far better place. Perhaps there will come a time when we understand this and go and just chew cud in the field like cows do instead of wanting to slit each other's throats. Human life is very precious - it's like a million miracles all in one.

Ronald Biggs

BLESSED *is the man who walks not in the counsel of the wicked, nor stands in the way of sinners, nor sits in the seat of scoffers; but his delight is in the law of the Lord, and on his law he meditates day and night. He is like a tree planted by streams of water, that yields its fruit in its season and its leaf does not wither. In all that he does, he prospers.*

Psalm 1:1-3

THE Christian ideal has not been tried and found wanting, it has been found difficult and left untried.

G.K. Chesterton

Mad Christians would walk around outside my gigs with placards saying Billy Idol is the Next Anti-Christ, which was stupid because my lyrics support love and gorgeousness.
< Billy Idol, singer.

ONLY THE DISCIPLES SEE THE RISEN ONE. ONLY BLIND FAITH HAS SIGHT THERE.
Dietrich Bonhoeffer

*Why should one be a Christian?
In order to be fully human.*
Hans Küng, theologian.

Most Christians are thermometers that record or register the temperature of majority opinion, not thermostats that transform and regulate the temperature of society.
Martin Luther King

I was the best Christian I could be in the world that I lived in with my temptations and failings. I often quote a Roy Orbison line, ❝*A diamond is a diamond, a stone is a stone, Man is part good, part bad*❞ that's me.
Johnny Cash, singer.

Christianity is the only co-operative society that exists for the benefit of non-members.

William Temple

Christianity has died many times and risen again; for it had a god who knew the way out of the grave.

G.K. Chesterton

MANY Christians are only "Christaholics" and not disciples at all. Disciples are cross-bearers; they seek Christ. Disciples dare to discipline themselves and the demands they place on themselves leave them enjoying the happiness of their growth. Christaholics are escapists looking for a short-cut to nirvana. Like drug addicts, they are trying to "bomb out" of their depressing world.

THERE is no automatic joy. Christ is not a happiness capsule; he is the way to the Father. But the way to the Father is not a carnival ride in which we sit and do nothing while we are whisked through various spiritual sensations.

Calvin Miller, writer.

<u>For</u> the <u>Christian</u>, the <u>bottom</u> <u>line</u> <u>is</u> there is no bottom line.

Richard Foster, spiritual writer.

I keep a list of all Born Agains. All the old drug addicts, all the worst fornicators and sex maniacs, people who have blown their minds in one way or another - they've all become Born Again Christians.

Julie Burchill, journalist.

The Kingdom of God is creation healed.

Hans Küng

A Christian society is not going to arrive until most of us really want it: and we are not going to want it until we become fully Christian. I may repeat, ❛Do as you would be done by❜ until I am blue in the face, but I cannot really carry it out till I love my neighbour as myself, till I learn to love God; and I cannot learn to love God except by learning to obey him. And so we are driven on to something more inward, driven on from social matters to religious matters. For the longest way round is the shortest way home.

C.S. Lewis

The second I met Mother Teresa she struck me as being the living embodiment of moral good. I felt I had no business sitting beside this tiny giant. There was no false modesty about here and there was a certainty of purpose which left her little patience. But she was totally selfless; every moment her aim seemed to be how can I use this or that situation to help others. She was never pious about this...

She is one of the few people who have impressed me on sight. I was in awe of her. She held my hand as she left and said, 'Remember this, I can do something you can't do and you can do something I can't do. But we both have to do it.'

< *Bob Geldof*

To give and not to count the cost;
fight and not to heed the
wounds;
toil and not to seek for rest;
labour and not ask for any
reward;
Save that of knowing that we do Thy
will.

St Ignatius Loyola

WHY DO BORN-AGAIN PEOPLE SO OFTEN MAKE YOU WISH THEY'D NEVER BEEN BORN IN THE FIRST PLACE?

Katharine Whitehorn, journalist.

Every Christian needs two conversions, first to Christ then to the world.

The Elder Blumhardt, writer.

Therefore, since we are surrounded by such a great cloud of witnesses, let us throw off everything that hinders and the sin that so easily entangles, and let us run with perseverance the race marked out for us. Let us fix our eyes on Jesus, the author and perfecter of our faith, who for the joy set before him endured the cross, scorning its shame, and sat down at the right hand of the throne of God. Consider him who endured such opposition from sinful men, so that you will not grow weary and lose heart.

Writer to the Hebrew Christians (12:1ff, NIV)

If you believe Jesus is the Light of the World there are two kinds of songs you can write - you can write songs about the Light or about what you see by the Light.

T. Bone Burnett

Evangelism is just ✎ one beggar ☎ telling another ✉ beggar where ☛ to find food.

D.T. Niles, minister.

I fear that Christians who stand with only one leg upon earth also stand with only one leg in Heaven.

Dietrich Bonhoeffer

The Christian ideal changed and reversed everything so that, as the gospel puts it, 'That which was exalted among men has become an abomination in the sight of God.' The ideal is no longer the greatness of Pharaoh or of a Roman emperor, not the beauty of a Greek nor the wealth of Phoenicia, but humility, purity, compassion, love. The hero is no longer Dives, but Lazarus the beggar; not Mary Magdalene in the day of her beauty but the day of her repentance; not those who acquire wealth but those who have abandoned it; not those who dwell in palaces but those who dwell in catacombs and huts; not those who rule over others but those who acknowledge no authority but God's.

Leo Tolstoy, writer.

To be *like Christ is a Christian.*

William Penn, Quaker.

It seems to me that the Christian life, when properly lived, is a rhythmic alternation between turning toward God in worship and running toward the world in love and with a passion for justice, between congregation and dispersal, liturgy and labour, worship and work, adoration and obedience.

Nicholas Wolterstorff, philosopher.

The chief contribution of Protestantism to human thought is its massive proof that God is a bore.

H.L. Mencken

14: CHURCH, WORSHIP, SERMONS AND BORING STUFF LIKE THAT

To all things clergic, I am allergic

Alexander Woollcott, writer.

Go to church this Sunday - avoid the Christmas rush.

Graffiti

A lot of the reason why I go to church is that my wife is in charge of the church choir and so I'm on parade. I'm not that good a churchgoer or Christian. I find it difficult to believe when one sees so much suffering and pain. But whether one believes or not in our Lord, if all he's done is bring us remarkable music and paintings then I'm very glad He came.

Jeffrey Archer, novelist.

POLICE cancelled a Sunday morning worship service in the town of Mount Clemens after fighting broke out in the congregation over who should be pastor at the Greater Morning Star Baptist Church. Five police officers were called to break up the disturbance during a service in which two rival ministers, the Rev Nathaniel Calhoun and the Rev Clarenton Bullock, stood in the pulpit using separate microphones. While Calhoun led his group of church members in the reading of Psalm 122, Bullock and his followers tried to outshout them with a reading of Psalm 92.

UNDER an agreement negotiated between the factions, each group's minister was supposed to take alternate Sundays. It was Bullock's turn but Calhoun told the congregation he was claiming the pulpit 'because I was elected your pastor and I'm supposed to preach'. It was then that the fighting broke out.

The test of a preacher is that his congregation goes away saying not,
"What a lovely sermon!"
but
"I will do something."

St Francis de Sales

To have played jazz in a church would have been an abomination. If I go into a church I'm deadly serious. Everybody has to stand alone at the time of judgement.

Ray Charles, singer.

Politics and church are the same thing - they keep the people in ignorance.

Bob Marley >

The work of a Beethoven and the work of a charwoman become spiritual on precisely the same condition, that of being offered to God, of being done humbly, ❛ as to the Lord ❜.
C.S. Lewis

It was being brought up in the church that got me into nude work and show business - I loved acting in those church plays. My childhood was spent in big cold vicarages; we didn't have much money but my father opened the door to everyone for tea and hospitality. I always remember being patted on the head by visiting bishops. My dad wasn't upset by my career; he would be more concerned if I was rude to my mother or caught shoplifting.

Fiona Richmond, former nude model and novelist.

The only statistic I can ever remember is that if all the people who go to sleep in church were laid end to end they would be a lot more comfortable.

Attributed to Queen Victoria.

I repeat what I told you once before when we feared we might be left without a radio station: God's best microphone is Christ and Christ's best microphone is the Church, and the Church is all of you. Let each one of you, in your own job, in your own vocation - nun, married person, bishop, priest, high school or university student, workman, labourer, market woman - each one in your own place live the faith intensely and feel that in your surroundings you are a true microphone of God our Lord.

Oscar Romero

The British churchgoer prefers a severe preacher because he thinks a few home truths will do his neighbour no harm.

George Bernard Shaw

I like the silent church before the service begins better than any preaching.

Ralph Waldo Emerson, philosopher.

I was a preacher one time. Scared the pants off every congregation.

Jerry Lee Lewis, singer.

Being raised in a vicarage is really good practice for a writer or anyone interested in comedy - you get to pick up a lot of medical and death jokes from doctors and undertakers. There was quite an emphasis on education in our home; vicarages are traditionally full of books. I also picked up from my father an interest in performing in public and writing my own scripts. Children of clergymen have a unique experience of growing up with people who are generally dedicated to looking after their fellow men.

John Wells, actor and writer.

PERHAPS THE MOST LASTING PLEASURE IN LIFE IS THE PLEASURE OF NOT GOING TO CHURCH.

William Inge

Visiting in his parish one day, a clergyman knocked at the door of one church member but got no reply. He was annoyed because he could hear footsteps and knew that the mother of the family was there. He left his visiting card, writing on it, 'Revelation 3.20: *"Behold I stand at the door and knock; if anyone hears my voice and opens the door I will come to him."*' The next Sunday, as the parishioners filed out of church after the service, the woman who had refused to open the door handed the vicar her card with 'Genesis 3, 10' written on it. Later, he looked up the passage, *'I heard the sound of thee in the garden and was afraid, because I was naked and I hid myself.'*

William Hinson, minister.

The Church is like the Red Cross in wartime. It keeps life from degenerating into a consistent inhumanity, but it does not materially alter the fact of the struggle itself.
Reinhold Niebuhr, theologian.

In the midst of bloody persecution under Idi Amin's rule in Uganda, a missionary society in England wrote to a bishop there, 'What can we send your people?' The answer came back: 'Not food, not medicine, 250 clerical collars.' This was the explanation: 'It is your Western prejudice which thinks this an odd request. You must understand, when our people are being rounded up to be shot, they must be able to spot their priests.'
Paul Seabury, writer.

OUR *society makes us out of touch with ourselves. The churches are finished; we don't have a pow-wow, a place to be emotional. The closest we have to that is a really great concert. There's an identification: the person on stage is supposed to express how they feel and the audience get it, they can weep, dance, go beserk, whatever they like. I think that's important. Singers are shamanistic in a funny sort of way.*

Annie Lennox, singer. **>**

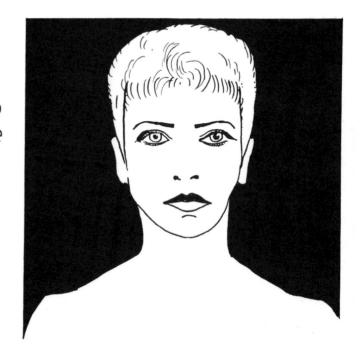

Geese in flock have seventy per cent greater range than a single goose on its own; geese in formation fly seventy five percent faster than single geese.

Ron Ferguson, minister.

A visitor to a Cardiff church admired the altar flowers. Agreeing on their beauty, the verger added, **"*On Sunday nights they are always given to those who are sick after the sermon.*"**

'Daily Telegraph' newspaper.

It seems to me easier to give sermons than to sit through them.

Lionel Blue, rabbi and broadcaster.

Classmates tend to set you apart at school if you are the son of a minister or priest so you begin to think you're different. My father was a Congregational minister and listening to him preach was important to my development: it was one of the things that made me believe in the validity of the leading article in the newspaper. There is a lot in common between old-fashioned preaching and journalism, though there is no pastoral work in the latter, thank God.

Simon Jenkins, editor, 'The Times' newspaper.

The Church which is married to the spirit of its age will be a widow in the next.

William Inge

*A**t the Harvest Festival in church the area behind the pulpit was piled high with tins of IXL fruit for the old-age pensioners. We had collected the tinned fruit from door to door. Most of it came from old-age pensioners.*

Clive James, writer.

THE CHURCH MUST BE REMINDED THAT IT IS NOT THE MASTER OR SERVANT OF THE STATE, BUT RATHER THE CONSCIENCE OF THE STATE.

Martin Luther King

The Church is an anvil that has worn out many hammers.

English proverb

The church is, and will continue to be, persecuted as long as it does not accommodate itself to the whims of totalitarianism whether of the right or of the left.

Arturo Rivera y Damas, Archbishop of San Salvador.

The new Archbishop of Canterbury had her excesses.

My *father was a Methodist minister, which gave me a happy, stable childhood. It was strict by today's standards, no Sunday newspapers for example. I had to go across the road to read the football results. There were no sermonettes in the Frost household, though we were taught that everyone has the duty to use their talents. My parents never laid on me the idea of going into the Church and were quite happy when I swapped congregations for audiences. I have kept many Christian beliefs. I also hate time-wasting. People say that is 'very Methodist'. It's true.*

David Frost, broadcaster.

Forgive us for turning our churches into private clubs; for loving familiar hymns and religious feelings more than we love You; for pasting stained glass on our eyes and our ears to shut out the cry of the hungry and the hurt of the world.

United Presbyterian Church, Litany for Holy Communion, 1968.

There are not many people who would care to sleep in a church. I don't mean at sermon time but at night and alone.

Charles Dickens, novelist.

The identification of a Church and a state is about as farcical as a vegetarian joining the Butchers Union.

Malcolm Muggeridge

we need to be the kind of church which tries to understand and obey the word of God for both rich and poor. The Church is one of the few bridges which can reach across to different sides of our polarized community. It is part of our reconciling task to help different groups to listen to what the others perceive to be happening.

Bishop David Sheppard

An inscription over a church door in Cheshire:

❖

"THIS IS THE HOUSE OF GOD. THIS IS THE GATE OF HEAVEN. (This door is locked in the winter months.)"

❖

'Daily Telegraph' newspaper.

A great many more people would want to go to church if there was a law against it.

Anon.

A church in Houston, USA, has introduced tithing by credit card. 'We believe the contributions will be made more promptly because people usually pay their credit card bills and then wonder if they have any left over,' said Rev Ed Peterman, Minister of Christ the King Lutheran Church.

'Now they can put their pledge on credit card and pay it later.'

He said there had been some initial fears that the move 'might be considered too commercial' but that the church went ahead to give members a 'third opportunity' to give, in addition to cash or cheques.

The 19th annual flower festival was on everyone's mind.

Why should we not alter to our use, quite humbly and dispassionately, a saying of St Augustine's:

66 Many whom God has, the church does not have; and many whom the church has, God does not have. 99

Karl Rahner, theologian.

It's a bit depressing if most of the congregation are in the churchyard instead of the church.

Alan Ayckbourn, playwright.

There is little good in filling churches with people who go out exactly the same as they came in; the call of the Church is not to fill churches but to fill heaven.
Fr Andrew SDC.

The British churchman goes to church as he goes to the bathroom, with the minimum of fuss and no explanation if he can help it.
Ronald Blythe, writer.

The Church of England is the perfect church for people who don't go to church.
Gerald Priestland, broadcaster.

Christianity was not founded by clergymen.
Norman Vincent Peale, writer.

The clergyman is expected to be a kind of human Sunday.
Samuel Butler

Sermons remain one of the last forms of public discourse where it is culturally forbidden to talk back.
Harvey Cox, writer.

A chap rang up the church office one Monday morning and asked, 'Who's the head hog at the trough?' 'Well,' gasped the church secretary, 'We hardly refer to the Right Reverend Smith in that manner.' The man continued, 'I don't care what you call him, I have a cheque for $10,000 and I want to know where to send it. Who's the head hog at the trough?' 'Oh,' the woman chirped. 'Here comes the big pig down the hall now.'

The Wittenberg Door Magazine

He who is near the church is often far from God.

French proverb

Once in seven years I burn all my sermons for it is a shame if I cannot write better sermons now than I did seven years ago.

John Wesley, founder of Methodism.

THE CHURCH IS LIKE A BAG OF CHIPS: TO BE TAKEN WITH A LARGE PINCH OF SALT, BUT AT ITS BEST, BRILLIANT.

Anon.

A missionary is someone who teaches cannibals to say grace before they eat him.

Anon.

We do not want as the newspapers say, a Church that *will move with* the world.

What we want is a Church *that will move* the world.

G.K. Chesterton

The problem with the Church today is not corruption. It is not institutionalism. No, the problem is far more serious than something like the minister running away with the organist. The problem is pettiness. Blatant pettiness.

Mike Yaconelli, minister and writer.

A church is a hospital for sinners, not a museum for saints.

Abigail Van Buren, writer.

15: FAITH, HOPE, DOUBT AND LOVE

You can do very little with faith, but you can do nothing without it.

Samuel Butler

FAITH is much better than belief. Belief is when someone else does the thinking.

R. Buckminster Fuller, writer.

He was of the faith, chiefly in the sense that the Church he currently did not attend was Catholic.

Kingsley Amis, novelist.

Faith is what we believe in but cannot prove. Superstition is what other people believe in but cannot prove.

Lambert Jeffries, writer.

The experience of losing your faith is an experience that, in the long run, belongs to faith.

Flannery O'Connor

Now faith is being sure of what we hope for and certain of what we do not see. By faith we understand that the universe was formed at God's command, so that what is seen was not made out of what was visible.

Writer to the Hebrew Christians (11:1,3 NIV)

Doubts are the ants in the pants of faith. They keep us alive and moving.

Frederich Buechner

Love is a fan club with only two fans.

Adrian Henri, poet.

Love is two minutes
fifty-two seconds of
squishing noises.
It shows your mind
isn't clicking right.

Johnny Rotten >

Faith may be defined briefly as an illogical belief in the occurrence of the improbable.

H.L. Mencken

Doreen's cross-cultural witness had yet to bear fruit in Bognor.

Faith is a conscious choice and I think I am on the verge of making the leap of faith. I wouldn't say that I have a specifically defined doctrine but it goes very deep. That doesn't mean I can start out my day saying the Lord's Prayer and end my day singing a chant. There is something. I don't know if it's Big Daddy or what but we are here for a reason.

William Hurt, actor.

The violence we preach is not the violence of the sword, the violence of hatred. It is the violence of love, of brotherhood, the violence that wills to beat weapons into sickles for work.

Oscar Romero

In the factory we manufacture cosmetics. In the store, we sell hopes.

Charles Revlon, cosmetics manufacturer.

How can I believe in God when just last week I got my tongue caught in the roller of an electric typewriter?

Woody Allen

❝ Faith is work. It is a struggle. You must struggle with all your heart. And on the way God will ambush you. ❞

Walter Wangerin, novelist.

Through violence you may murder the hater, but you do not murder the hate.

Martin Luther King

Don't curse the darkness: light a candle.

Chinese proverb

Man is a credulous animal and must believe something. In the absence of good grounds for belief, he will be satisfied with bad ones.

Bertrand Russell, philosopher.

If I speak in the tongues of men and of angels but have not love, I am only a resounding gong or a clanging cymbal. If I have the gift of prophecy and can fathom all mysteries and all knowledge, and if I have a faith that can move mountains, but have not love, I am nothing. If I give all I possess to the poor and surrender my body to the flames, but have not love, I gain nothing.

Love is patient, love is kind. It does not envy, it does not boast, it is not proud. It is not rude, it is not self-seeking, it is not easily angered, it keeps no record of wrongs. Love does not delight in evil but rejoices with the truth. It always protects, always trusts, always hopes, always perseveres.

ove never fails. But where there are prophecies, they will cease; where there are tongues, they will be stilled; where there is knowledge, it will pass away. For we know in part and we prophesy in part, but when perfection comes, the imperfect disappears. When I was a child, I talked like a child, I thought like a child, I reasoned like a child. When I became a man, I put childish ways behind me. Now we see but a poor reflection as in a mirror, then we shall see face to face. Now I know in part, then I shall know fully, even as I am fully known.

nd now these three remain: faith, hope and love. But the greatest of these is love.

Paul in his first letter to the Corinthian Church (ch.13, NIV)

love is only the dirty trick played on us to achieve the continuation of the species.

Somerset Maugham, novelist and playwright.

To be commanded to love God at all, let alone in the wilderness, is like being commanded to be well when we are sick, to sing for joy when we are dying of thirst, to run when our legs are broken. But this is the first and great commandment nonetheless. Even in the wilderness, especially in the wilderness, you shall love Him.

Frederich Buechner

Love conquers all things except poverty and faith.

Mae West

We have not lost faith but we have transferred it from God to the medical profession.

George Bernard Shaw